HILLARY RODHAM CLINTON

DO ALL THE GOOD YOU CAN

HILLARY RODHAM CLINTON

DO ALL THE GOOD YOU CAN

CYNTHIA LEVINSON

Balzer + Bray
An Imprint of HarperCollins*Publishers*

Balzer + Bray is an imprint of HarperCollins Publishers.

Hillary Rodham Clinton: Do All the Good You Can
Copyright © 2016 by Cynthia Levinson

Library of Congress Control Number: 2015940617
ISBN 978-0-06-238729-5 (trade paperback)
ISBN 978-0-06-238730-1 (hardcover)

Typography by Aurora Parlagreco
15 16 17 18 19   CG/OPM   10 9 8 7 6 5 4 3 2 1

First Edition

To the many accomplished women in Davis Hall,
1964–67

CONTENTS

....

HILLARY RODHAM CLINTON

DO ALL THE GOOD YOU CAN

PROLOGUE

. . . .

Star student.

   Spokesperson for her generation.

   Advocate for children, women, and families.

   Corporate lawyer.

   First Lady of Arkansas.

   First Lady of the United States.

   Health-care reformer.

   US senator.

   Secretary of state.

   Two-time presidential candidate.

   President of the United States?

   These achievements—and even more—seem impossible for one person to accomplish in sixty-eight years. But Hillary Rodham Clinton has managed all of them. Is she some kind of superwoman?

Yes. And no.

She started life like lots of kids, made wise decisions and wretched ones, glowed with success and suffered humiliating setbacks. Like lunging for the next ring that dangles from playground crossbars and then the next and the next, Hillary has kept reaching.

. . . .

A NOTE ON NAMES

Like a rock star, Hillary is a one-name phenomenon. Her staff respectfully calls her "the First Lady" or "the Senator" or "Madam Secretary," depending on when they worked for her. In this book, I refer to her as Hillary because that's how she identifies herself. (On the telephone, she sometimes says, "Hi, it's Hillary!") Also, since her supporters declare that they're "Ready for Hillary," that's how the public knows her.

On the other hand, even friends call her husband "Mr. President." But because this is Hillary's story and she calls him Bill, so do I.

. . . .

CHAPTER 1

A Midwestern Girl in Mid-Century America
1947–1965

. . . .

"My Immediate World Seemed Safe and Stable"

When Hillary Diane Rodham was growing up, girls in Park Ridge, Illinois, did not wear jeans or shorts or T-shirts or sandals to school. They didn't wear pants, either, even on frigid days when icy winds swept across Lake Michigan and swirled through Chicago's northwestern suburbs. Instead, girls wore dresses or skirts, buttoned-up blouses, and, on their feet, black-and-white saddle oxfords or patent-leather Mary Janes with white socks neatly folded over. This was the proper look at Eugene Field Elementary School in the 1950s. And Hillary fit right in.

There was one way, though, that she stood out. No one else wore glasses like hers. They were as dense as the heavy bottom of a soda bottle and boldly rimmed in red frames, which emphasized her thick eyebrows. Other kids stared; her severely nearsighted eyes looked blurry through those lenses. So, Hillary sometimes took them off and let her friend Betsy Johnson lead her around school like a guide dog. Betsy had to whisper the names of people they passed in the hallway so Hillary could say hi.

There was another way that Hillary and her two younger brothers, Hughie and Tony, fit in. Like the other children at school, they were white and Christian. As far as she could tell, no Jewish, Asian, Hispanic, or black people lived in Park Ridge, and they would have been discouraged if they tried to move in. Hardly any schools or neighborhoods in the entire country were racially integrated.

They were, however, bustling with children. Born on October 26, 1947, Hillary was part of a "baby boom"— a dramatic increase in the number of children born during the late 1940s as American soldiers returned home following the end of World War II. The square block on which the Rodhams lived boasted forty-seven youngsters!

Hillary could dash out the door of their spacious, elm-shaded brick home and round up a flock of kids for pickup basketball, football, or softball. In winter, they played ice hockey on a rink created by a neighbor who flooded his backyard with his garden hose.

Every summer, the Rodhams spent two weeks at a rustic lakefront cabin that Hillary's father and grandfather had built in Pennsylvania's Pocono Mountains. With no hot water indoors, they bathed in Lake Winola, where they also swam and fished. Hillary's father even taught her and her brothers to shoot, lining up tin cans for target practice.

Today, we might call Hillary an all-around athlete. Back then, hardly any girls played sports, and she was known as a tomboy. She learned from sports, she said, "You win one day, you lose the next day, you don't take it personally. You get up every day, and you go on."[1]

Hillary began to learn this lesson when she was barely four years old, shortly after the Rodhams moved from a one-bedroom apartment near downtown Chicago to Park Ridge. She ran into the house, wailing that a girl named Suzy, who lived across the street with her brothers, had shoved her.

"There's no room in this house for cowards," her mother proclaimed. "You're going to have to stand up to her. The next time she hits you, I want you to hit her back."[2]

Hillary didn't wait to get hit. She crossed the street, punched Suzy—to her brothers' astonishment—and reported to her mother, "I can play with the boys now!"[3]

Mostly, though, Hillary kept the peace and obeyed grown-ups. She sat enthralled when her mother read and reread Dr. Seuss. Her favorite lines were, "You have brains in your head. You have feet in your shoes. You can steer yourself any direction you choose."[4] Hillary chose to strive. While her brothers looked forward to the family's annual outing to Kiddieland for roller-coaster rides, she preferred excursions to Chicago's Field Museum, where she studied baby mummies.

She brought home almost all As on her report card; earned about as many Brownie and Girl Scout merit badges as could fit on her sash; cocaptained her school's safety patrol; and organized backyard carnivals and a mock Olympics, from which the athletes collected a paper bag of money that they donated to United Way.

Hillary also prayed and went to Sunday school, Bible school, youth group, and altar guild at First United Methodist Church. Her mother taught at Sunday school. "We talked with God, walked with God, ate, studied, and argued with God," Hillary said. "Each night, we knelt by our beds to pray."[5] God sent sunbeams, she believed, directly to her.

Sometimes, though, Hillary learned traditional lessons the wrong way. In third grade, she hit a boy with a ruler because he had dinged her with a spitball. She thought the Golden Rule meant "Do unto others exactly what they did to you"[6]—instead of "Treat other people the way you would like to be treated."

Family lore had it that, in the eighteenth century, John Wesley himself, the founder of the faith, had converted Hillary's father's great-great-grandparents in southern Wales. Wesley charged his followers with a straightforward guideline: "Do all the good you can, by all the means you can, in all the ways you can, in all the places you can, at all the times you can, to all the people you can, as long as ever you can."

Hillary took this rule to heart and repeated it to herself, especially when she faced hard decisions. "Those are words I've tried to live by,"[7] she later said. Yet figuring out what was the good thing to do and the best way to do it would challenge her throughout her life.

For middle-class children like Hillary, the 1950s were a calm, orderly time. The Rodhams sat down to dinner every night at six o'clock. Hillary especially looked forward to her mother's mac and cheese or meat loaf with dill pickles. After dinner, her mother helped her with English and history homework. Her father, whom she called Pop-Pop, oversaw math. The next morning, he'd wake her up bellowing a favorite song, "Ain't We Got Fun?"

"My immediate world seemed safe and stable,"[8] Hillary recalled.

In fact, however, her home life was filled with strife. Both of Hillary's parents had suffered tough childhoods. Each tried to prepare and protect her in different ways.

"Sometimes He'd Get Carried Away"

The son of a poor immigrant and a local girl, her father, Hugh, attended college in Pennsylvania; however, he graduated in 1935, during the Great Depression, when jobs and money were scarce. Hugh worked in coal mines and for a company that manufactured lace. Anxious to do better, he rode freight cars, jumping on and off like a hobo, until he reached Chicago. There, he found a job selling curtains, and eventually started his own two-man company. Working fourteen hours a day, he designed, printed, measured, sewed, delivered, and hung curtains for hotels and banks.

During World War II, Hugh served in the navy, where he trained recruits headed for combat. Like a drill sergeant, he barked commands, accepted no excuses for failure, and refused to listen to anyone who disagreed with him.

Unfortunately for his wife and children, Hugh carried this strict military discipline, his fear of being poor, and his outsized pride in himself home with him every night. When Hillary got into a fix, he refused to help. Instead, he'd demand, "How are you going to dig yourself out of this one?"[9]

He didn't even praise her when she showed him a report card full of As. "That must be an easy school you go to,"[10] he'd tell her. She'd worked so hard! Some kids might have given up—but not Hillary.

Sometimes Hugh plopped the kids into his fancy Cadillac and drove them through Chicago's slums, not far from where Hillary and her parents had lived. He wanted them "to see what became of people who . . . lacked the self-discipline and motivation to keep their lives on track,"[11] he said. If these bums worked as hard as he did, Hugh suggested, they could be successful, like him. After all, he hadn't gotten a dime from anyone.

Unlike Hugh, Hillary's mother felt sorry for poor people. "Things happen to people that they have no control over,"[12] she pointed out. Dorothy had Hillary join her church youth group on Saturdays when the girls babysat for the children of the migrant farm workers who moved into a trailer camp west of Chicago every fall. The youngsters' parents and older siblings, some of whom were Hillary's classmates, spent the day picking the fruits and vegetables that corporations turned into bottled juice or canned soup.

One weekend, Hillary told her mother about a seven-year-old girl named Maria, who didn't have a dress to wear to her First Communion. The Rodhams bought her a dress.

"When we presented it to Maria's mother," Hillary said, "she started crying and dropped to her knees to kiss my mother's hands."[13]

Dorothy understood that these families worked hard for low pay and could use a helping hand.

"Where did you ever come up with such a stupid idea?" Hugh would fling back at Dorothy. "Miss Smarty-Pants!"[14] In retaliation, Dorothy called her husband "Mr. Difficult."[15]

Hillary's parents argued so often and so loudly that she covered her ears. And her father didn't stop at sarcastic, humiliating insults.

"Occasionally he got carried away when disciplining us, yelling louder or using more physical punishment . . . than I thought was fair,"[16] Hillary admitted.

Hugh turned off the heat in the house overnight and accused the children of going soft if they complained of the cold. He rarely allowed Hillary to buy new clothes, and she often felt out of fashion compared to her friends. When she asked for an allowance, he refused, saying, "I feed you, don't I?"[17]

From the time she was thirteen, she held jobs after school and over the summer babysitting, shoveling snow, picking weeds, and working as a salesgirl. When she turned sixteen and wanted to get a driver's license, he refused again, telling her she didn't need to drive a car because she had a bicycle. She got a license anyway, in secret, with the help of a friend.

Still, Hillary said, "He told us repeatedly that he would always love us."[18] She even thought she inherited her father's boisterous laugh.

"Do You Want to Be the Lead Actor in Your Life?"

Hillary's friend Betsy wondered why Dorothy didn't take the children and leave. Dorothy told Hillary that she did not believe in divorce unless the situation was dire. *"You do not leave the marriage,"*[19] she insisted.

Although Hillary didn't know it until she grew up, Dorothy's childhood had certainly been dire. Dorothy's mother (Hillary's grandmother) was only fifteen years old when her daughter was born. She neglected her, forcing Dorothy to scrounge for food from the time she was only three or four years old.

When Dorothy turned eight, her parents abandoned her and her three-year-old sister altogether. The girls rode a train, by themselves, for four days and nights from Chicago to Los Angeles, to stay with their grandmother. This woman, however, alternated between ignoring and punishing them. They were even forbidden from trick-or-treating on Halloween. When Dorothy went out one late-October night anyway, she was confined to her room for a year.

Dorothy vowed to treat her own children lovingly. Five years after she met and married Hugh, Hillary was born, and Dorothy kept her vow. A homemaker, like almost all of the other mothers in Park Ridge, she prepared peanut butter and jelly sandwiches on white bread—no crusts—when Hillary bicycled home from school at lunchtime. She once stayed up all night to sew an outfit for Hillary to wear in a school fashion show. Mother and daughter played cards and board games and lay beside each other on the grass, pointing out the shapes of passing clouds.

Dorothy couldn't buffer Hillary from Hugh's nasty insults and demands. But she shared what she had learned, hoping that her daughter would make better choices.

"Do you want to be the lead actor in your life," Dorothy would ask, "or a minor player who simply reacts to what others think you should say or do?"[20] Hillary absorbed but also struggled with her mother's lessons.

The "Red Menace" vs. the "University of Life"

When Hillary was thirteen and entered Maine East High School in 1961, she began to hear two other people, besides her parents, disagree with each other. One was her ninth-grade history teacher, Paul Carlson, who was tough-minded, like her father. The other was the new minister at First United Methodist Church, Reverend Don Jones, who was softhearted, like her mother. Both sounded convincing. But she knew one had to be wrong. Their views were as opposite as right and left.

"The Communist threat is a global one . . . In war there can be no substitute for victory."[21]

Mr. Carlson played a recording of this rousing speech

in which Army General Douglas MacArthur warned Congress about the dangers of Communism. Surrounded by the model warplanes and battle maps that decorated the classroom, Hillary agreed with Mr. Carlson, MacArthur, and her father: Communism—the "Red Menace"—threatened democracy.

COMMUNISM AND THE COLD WAR

For four decades after World War II, America was involved in a Cold War with the Soviet Union, China, and other eastern countries that had turned to Communism. Under this strict political and economic system, the government, rather than individuals, owns property and businesses. The government distributes what people need, such as housing and food. Also, religious practice is banned, and people are assigned to jobs and to locations. The Cold War between the East and the West consisted largely of propaganda, fearmongering, and spying.

His star pupil disappointed him one day, however. Repeating a common warning, Carlson announced,

"Better dead than red!" When Hillary's friend Ricky Ricketts whispered, "Well, I'd rather be alive," she got the giggles and was thrown out of class. Hillary worked her way back into her teacher's good graces by writing a seventy-five-page essay that argued for America's military might.

"Hillary was a hawk," her teacher proudly claimed—that is, someone who believes in going to war to keep the country strong.

"Heard one person starve, I heard many people laughin' . . . It's a hard rain's a-gonna fall."[22]

Reverend Jones, on the other hand, played a recording of a song by folksinger Bob Dylan. In Jones's twice-weekly "University of Life," Hillary's youth group analyzed the injustice of some people starving while others laughed. They visited with inner-city Hispanic and black kids, who shared stories about relatives who had been shot. Talking with people, she learned, was different from staring at them from inside her father's Cadillac.

"It just kind of opened up my mind,"[23] she said.

Jones spoke about the need for "faith in action"[24]—the idea that helping the poor and making America more fair was the Christian thing to do. Discussing what actions to take, the young people debated how to "do all the good" they could.

Concerned about social problems, Hillary's mother would approve of the minister's lessons. She also approved when Jones took the group to hear the civil rights leader Dr. Martin Luther King, Jr. speak in 1962. Calling his talk "Remaining Awake through a Revolution," King urged his listeners to integrate America.

"Our world is a neighborhood,"[25] he said. Everyone should share responsibility for it. That idea struck Hillary and stuck with her. After his talk, she stood in line to shake King's hand, capping what she later called "a moving, eye-opening, and formative experience."[26]

Hillary wasn't convinced, though, that the ministers and her mother were right. After all, her father and Mr. Carlson argued that the world wasn't a neighborhood. With Communism abroad and shootings at home, it was a dangerous place. Her father even considered King to be a troublemaker. The two sides—the minister versus the teacher—tussled with each other and over Hillary.

Jones later said, "We were fighting for her soul and her mind."[27]

He—and Hillary's mother—seemed to lose the fight around the time President John F. Kennedy was assassinated. On November 22, 1963, school was dismissed early, and Hillary came home to find her mother watching the sad news on television. Her mother confessed that, like Kennedy, she was a Democrat, one of the very few in Park Ridge. She'd never told Hugh. Hillary felt bad for the Kennedy family—but not bad enough to become a Democrat.

Hillary joined an anti-Communist club that Carlson organized. When he accused Jones of trying to brainwash the kids into being Communists, the youth minister had to leave his job. Nevertheless, Hillary stayed in touch with him and his message of faith and service.

Some kids might have found these opposing opinions confusing. Instead, Hillary said that she "learned that a person was not necessarily bad just because you did not agree with him, and that if you believed in something, you had better be prepared to defend it."[28]

Senior Year!

Because Maine East was overcrowded, Hillary was assigned to a new school, Maine South, for her senior year in 1964. For the first time, she attended a racially integrated school. The previous year, she had been elected vice president of her class, wrote for the school newspaper, and served as an alternate for her school's team when it appeared on a television quiz show.

Senior year, she ran for school president, even though a boy said it would be "really stupid if I thought a girl could be elected president."[29] She had received a similar response when she wrote to the National Aeronautics and Space Administration (NASA), to volunteer for astronaut training. Even though NASA was secretly testing women for space travel, the rejection letter stated that girls were not accepted into the program. She was outraged by the males at both NASA and Maine South.

Of course she could be elected, she believed! But she wasn't. Nevertheless, when the boy who won the election asked Hillary to help write the new school's constitution, she decided to be a good sport and do it. Sometimes, she realized, you have to swallow your pride and compromise.

That fall was a presidential election year. Senator Barry Goldwater, the conservative Republican nominee, was running against President Lyndon Baines Johnson, a Democrat. Hillary signed on to work as a "Goldwater Girl." At rallies, she wore a yellow flared skirt and neck bandanna, white blouse and wrist-length gloves, and a straw cowboy hat banded with the slogan "AuH_2O," the chemical symbols for "gold" and "water."

Hillary also convinced the school to hold a mock presidential debate. She planned to take the part of Goldwater, and her friend Ellen, the only Democrat she knew besides her mother, would play Johnson—but their teacher made them switch! She'd have to explain the Democrats' positions, which supported civil rights, health care, and programs for the poor. Hillary "went ballistic."[30]

"I resented every hour spent in the library reading the Democrats' platform,"[31] she said. At least, she discovered that Johnson was trying to stop the spread of Communism in Asia, particularly in a country called

Vietnam. When it came time for the debate, she and Ellen did it with "teeth gritted."[32] A photograph in the yearbook showed them posing good-naturedly with raised fists.

Hillary wasn't *all* about politics, though. Betsy suggested to a friend that he take Hillary to the senior prom. The boy, Jim, thought she was too serious to be any fun. So, to test her, he took her to the top of a long, winding driveway and handed her his skateboard. Although she'd never ridden one before, she hopped on, zigzagged to the bottom of the hill without wiping out, and earned the date. She could still play with the boys.

Convincing her father that she needed a new dress for the prom and convincing her unruly hair to behave remained problems, however. Looking dejectedly at the plain-Jane frock Hugh let her buy, she wrote to Reverend Jones, "everyone else next to me will think they are overdressed."[33] Perhaps, since her father didn't want her to date or go out dancing, he was hoping she would cancel, but with a blue bow holding back her hair, Hillary and Jim had a good time anyway.

HAIR HORROR

Hillary wrestled with her thick blond hair from the time she started high school. Usually, she just scrunched it into a ponytail. But, wanting a stylish pageboy or a flip for freshman year, she went to a hairdresser, who carelessly hacked a hunk of hair from the right side of her head and then, to make it even, whacked off a shank on the left. Hillary shrieked. To disguise the disaster, Hillary bought a fake ponytail and pinned it to the top of her head. The ruse worked until her friend Ricky tugged on it at school, and he ended up holding it in his hand. Mortified but polite, Ricky apologized.

"Thus began my lifelong hair struggles,"[34] Hillary has said.

Dueling messages at home and at school continued as she was deciding where to go to college. Near the top of her class, a National Merit Scholarship Finalist, and active in the newspaper, pep club, the spring musical, a variety show, and winner of the science award, Hillary had her choice of excellent schools. She couldn't apply to "the Ivies," like Yale or Princeton, because they accepted only men. But the "Seven Sisters" were their equivalents for intelligent, ambitious young women. One of her teachers advised Hillary to attend Smith College; another urged Wellesley.

"Learn to earn," her father said. That is, go to school to get a job.

Her mother, as usual, disagreed. "Learn to learn," she advised her daughter. That is, be curious and explore what interests you, even if it doesn't pay.

Photographs of Wellesley's Lake Waban reminded Hillary of summers at Lake Winola. So, in the fall of 1965, at age seventeen, she headed off to Wellesley, without ever having seen the place. She had some confidence, though. Hillary's high school classmates had voted her Most Likely to Succeed.

CHAPTER 2

East Coast School: Wellesley College
1965–1969

. . . .

"Wholesome Creatures"

In September 1965, Hillary Rodham and her parents drove a thousand miles east from Park Ridge, Illinois, to Wellesley, Massachusetts, a suburb of Boston. After detouring by mistake to scruffy-looking Harvard Square, they were pleased to enter Wellesley College's secluded five-hundred-acre campus, where they wound past spired brick buildings, an arboretum, and a stately library.

The Vil Junior, an upperclassman responsible for orienting freshmen, greeted them at Hillary's dormitory, Davis Hall, and directed them to her assigned room, a cozy single. Through the window of the room across the hallway, Hillary could gaze at Lake Waban, one of the reasons she had chosen to come to Wellesley.

Hearing music, Hillary wandered down the hall to ask another freshman what radio station she was listening to. Jinnet Fowles was unloading an entire station wagon's worth of belongings. She looked at Hillary's bare room and wondered, "How could anybody get to college with only two suitcases?!"[35] It wasn't long, though, before the two girls were trading clothes. She especially admired Hillary's navy-blue wool pea coat with matching felt helmet.

Hillary received her freshman green beanie, which she was expected to wear for college-wide Stepsinging at the chapel, and the college's rule book. Friday and Saturday night curfews: a choice of eleven p.m. one night or one a.m. the other. No gentleman callers allowed in rooms except between two p.m. and five thirty p.m. on Sundays. Skirts required for dinner.

She pored over the course catalog, calculating the complicated distribution requirements needed to graduate. Two classes in literature, two in the arts, four in science, and more—a heavy load of ten subjects every year. The documents also reminded students of the college motto: *Non Ministrari sed Ministrare.* "Not to be ministered unto, but to minister." This notion of service to others felt right to Hillary, a confirmed Methodist and already an activist.

The Rodhams could feel secure knowing that Hillary would pass the next four years in this safe haven. As *Time* magazine wrote that fall about the Class of '69, "They are simply wholesome creatures, unencumbered by the world's woes, who make normal, well-adjusted housewives."[36] Even so, Dorothy cried for much of the return trip to Park Ridge. And just weeks later, Hillary called her parents to say she wanted to come home.

"I didn't think I was smart enough to be there,"[37] she said. Her French professor told her, "Mademoiselle, your talents lie elsewhere."[38] Where were her talents? she wondered. How could a National Merit Finalist not be smart enough, even for this competitive college?

Almost half of Hillary's classmates had graduated from private schools where the work was more demanding than at Maine South. About a fifth of her class was composed of legacies—children and grandchildren of Wellesley grads, who knew what to expect.

Hillary found Wellesley "all very rich and fancy and very intimidating."[39]

For once, Hugh didn't ask his daughter how she planned to dig herself out. He told her she could leave. Dorothy, however, said she didn't want quitters any more than she wanted cowards in the family. Hillary decided to stay and make the best of things.

"I Wonder Who Is Me?"

Knowing that college offers a time to experiment, Hillary tried on "different personalities and lifestyles,"[40] or at least outfits. Her friend Kris Olson called them her "costumes."[41] Inside, Hillary pondered, "I wonder who is me?"[42]

Self-conscious about her bottle-bottom glasses, she tried contact lenses. But they were heavy and hard and kept slipping out of place. Figuring there was no alternative, she turned her glasses into a fashion statement and ordered a variety of colorful frames.

One month, determined to be a scholar, Hillary spent every possible minute studying. Comfy in fluffy slippers and striped pajamas, she hunkered down in her room with books, emerging only for meals and classes. She gave up that identity when her "diet [of reading and writing] gave me indigestion."[43]

Another month, she adopted a hippie look. She wore bell-bottom jeans and a purple floppy hat over long, straight hair, which she parted down the middle like the folksinger Judy Collins. She later allowed an artist who lived in the dorm, Laura Grosch, to paint a flower on her chin.

Generally, though, she didn't pay much attention to what she wore. She told a friend that she had bought a pair of clunky, square-toed boots because "I felt sorry for them."[44]

Clothing wasn't nearly so important to Hillary as action. Not long after classes started, she took Karen Williamson, who was one of only six black students in their class, to church in the town of Wellesley. This was a daring act in a community where there were few black residents other than maids. Perhaps Hillary remembered that Dr. King had told the crowd in Chicago that the most segregated time of the week is eleven a.m. on Sunday, when black people and white people head to different churches.

After the service, she excitedly called her parents. They scolded her for using a religious ceremony to make a political point about racial integration.

"I was so disappointed in their reaction," she wrote Reverend Jones. "My attitudes toward so many things have changed in just three weeks."[45]

Not so much, though, that she was ready to switch political parties. Elected president of the college's Young Republicans Club her freshman year, Hillary rallied members to support Republican candidates. Anyone "who doesn't want to go out and shake hands can type letters or do general office work,"[46] she urged. Among the candidates they helped was the attorney general of Massachusetts, Edward Brooke, a black man who was running for US Senate.

"Negroes with Negroes"

Karen and the other black members of their class noticed that all but one of them was assigned either a black roommate or a single room. Wellesley's housing was segregated! This was not just insulting; people were beginning to argue that it should be against the law.

To protest, the ten black students on campus confronted the administration, which responded that it was college policy to room "Jews with Jews, Negroes with Negroes, Chinese with Chinese."[47] Furious, the students wrote articles in the literary magazine and newspaper.

Hillary's boyfriend, a junior at Harvard College named Geoffrey, had a roommate who was black. Clearly, Wellesley's dorm policy was old-fashioned. Although she enjoyed dancing with Geoff to the latest Beatles album, she preferred to talk about issues in the *New York Times*, a liberal newspaper she'd started reading. As they talked, she learned more about the civil rights movement. So many brave people, including students, were demanding their rights.

In 1963, when Hillary was in tenth grade, thousands of black kids marched in Birmingham, Alabama, to end segregation. She watched Dr. King on television as he told a quarter-million marchers in Washington, DC, "I have a dream." The following year, President Johnson strong-armed Congress to pass the Civil Rights Act of 1964, which outlawed racial discrimination. In the spring of Hillary's senior year of high school, state troopers beat marchers in Selma, Alabama. The month before she left for college, Johnson signed the Voting Rights Act of 1965.

All of these events had hit the news. But in college, Hillary was becoming more aware and concerned. She and several white students formed an organization, Wellesley Against Racism (WAR).

Segregation was one of several national issues that caught her attention.

Women's Lib

In 1963, two years before Hillary arrived on campus, a woman named Betty Friedan published a book called *The Feminine Mystique*. The book argued that American women were unhappy because they were expected—and often permitted—to be only housewives and mothers, not professional working people. By the next year, the book was the bestselling paperback—and one of the most talked-about books—in America.

Friedan's work helped jump-start the Women's Liberation Movement, especially two years later when she founded the National Organization for Women (NOW). Members urged women to trade in their aprons for business suits and challenged companies that discriminated against female employees. A Wellesley dropout started a more radical group, the Women's International Terrorist Conspiracy from Hell (WITCH). The group staged protests and burned their bras near the Miss America pageant.

Hillary and her friends did not protest. They didn't need to. The all-female college gave them the chance to run things—everything, in fact, from the newspaper to the dance studio—without competition from men. As a friend of Hillary's said, "We were gaining confidence that we could do something—as women."[48]

Today, most mothers work at jobs outside their home. In 1965, less than one-third did so, and these working mothers were often criticized. A panel of doctors warned in an article in *Life* magazine, "the disease of working women leads to children who become juvenile delinquents, atheists, Communists, and homosexuals."[49] Holding a job wasn't an accomplishment, these doctors asserted. It was a medical condition!

Most Wellesley girls didn't share this opinion. But they weren't sure if or how they could "have it all"— marriage, family, and a career.

'Nam

From 1940 to 1973, young men in America were subject to be drafted into military service. As the war in Vietnam heated up, more and more were inducted. In 1965, troop levels there hit nearly two hundred thousand—and two years later, almost half a million.

Hillary believed that President Johnson was right to send troops across the Pacific Ocean to fight Communism. Otherwise, dominoes might fall: if North Vietnam overran South Vietnam, all of Southeast Asia could turn Communist and gang up on the United States. She wanted a strong America, as Mr. Carlson had taught.

On the other hand, she found the war unjust. Americans watched battles on television and were appalled by what they saw—horrific injuries, US soldiers murdering Vietnamese women and children, planes dumping poison on farmers and their fields. And there was no sign of victory, no light at the end of the tunnel.

Men who resisted, by burning their draft card or failing to appear for induction, could be jailed. Some fled to Canada, not knowing if they'd ever be able to return home. Others deferred service by staying in school as long as possible.

Hillary had a new boyfriend, David, who avoided the draft by being recognized as a conscientious objector, meaning that he was morally opposed to all wars. Actions such as these led her to wonder, "Were you being unpatriotic if you used the system of deferments . . . to avoid fighting?"[50]

Young people held marches, demonstrations, sit-ins, hunger strikes, and teach-ins to persuade Johnson to bring the troops home. They chanted, "Hell no! We won't go!" They sang, "All we are saying is give peace a chance," the anthem of the antiwar movement composed by John Lennon, a member of the Beatles. Dr. King spoke out against the war, declaring, "This madness must cease."[51] People even set themselves on fire to protest America's actions.

"My friends and I constantly discussed and debated it," Hillary said. "It was agonizing for everyone. I spent countless hours wrestling with my own contradictory feelings."[52]

Along the way, she resigned from the Young Republicans Club; however, she didn't yet consider herself a Democrat. An outdoorsy friend said, "She had her feet in two canoes."[53] In a quandary about her political beliefs, Hillary asked Reverend Jones, "Can one be a mind conservative and a heart liberal?"[54]

"The Hill"—A Leader and a Friend

During sophomore year, Hillary was elected to the student senate. She strode into office determined to eliminate those burdensome course requirements.

To solicit support for the change, Hillary worked both ends—the grassroots student level and the top administrators. Attacking graduation provisions, she gathered a crowd one afternoon by distributing posters that read, "Forum on DISTRIBUTION REQUIREMENTS. Tuesday 12:45. MANDATORY." In smaller type, the poster continued, "for all interested students & faculty."[55] Standing behind a snowbank on the steps of Founders Hall, Hillary gave a speech to a hundred or so chilly but attentive students and professors.

"Hillary revealed her genius of saying exactly what was in our minds and hearts at the right moment," Laura said.

With support from faculty and students, she went to see Wellesley president Ruth Adams. Adams discovered that Hillary "could be very insistent!"[56] Understanding the power of the press in influencing opinions, Hillary also involved the editor of the college newspaper. By the end of the year, the rule book got a lot thinner.

Laura told her, "I have always had the idea that a woman could be president . . . You are that person."[57] That was not the last time Hillary heard that prediction from her peers.

The next year, Hillary was named a Vil Junior and tapped to lead the group, a prestigious honor. She was popular with other students, who found her exuberant, curious, and earnest. "Hillary's guffaw echoed down the hallway,"[58] a friend recalled.

She made up funny nicknames—like "Peacharooni"— for her friends and referred to herself as "the Hill."[59] She cheered up glum dorm-mates with hand-drawn greeting cards that included her personal logo—a figure looking over a fence. They trooped to mixers—dances to which the college bused in guys from Harvard and Yale. To one, she wore a "costume" of bright orange floor-length culottes with feathers.

Hillary also tutored an underprivileged child in Boston. This was a way she could fulfill the college motto of providing service. Of course, she kept up her grades.

When the professor of her psychology course lost her lecture notes, she asked Hillary for the notes she'd taken! Alan Schechter, one of her favorite professors in her major—political science—said, "She was very organized and articulate and goal-oriented."[60] Hillary found that she had many talents.

Near the end of junior year, Hillary ran for president of the College Government Association. Unlike high school, there were no boys to defeat her this time, but she had two opponents. Drawing on her experience campaigning for Republican candidates, she went door-to-door in every dorm to ask students for votes and for their opinions about problems on campus.

When Hillary learned that she had won, she exclaimed to a professor, "I can't believe what just happened! I was just elected president of the government."[61]

Perhaps she couldn't believe it but, having listened to the voters, she was ready to serve. During her presidency, she worked with other students to convince the administration to scrap other rules that limited students' choices. Curfews especially annoyed them because they were grown up enough to decide for themselves how late to stay out. This was an issue of women's rights!

By the end of her term as college government president, those regulations were gone, too.

No previous Wellesley class had done so much to improve students' social and academic lives.

Having honed her persuasive skills on domestic campus matters, Hillary spread her activism to concerns beyond the college.

1968: A "Watershed Year"

In 1968, Hillary completed junior year and began senior year. One shocking event after another bombarded America that year like a rat-a-tat-tat machine gun, shaking the previously staid Wellesley campus.

JANUARY 31: Communist North Vietnam overtook South Vietnam. US forces were overwhelmed. More Americans clamored to end the war.

MARCH 12: Antiwar presidential candidate Eugene McCarthy nearly defeated incumbent President Johnson in New Hampshire's Democratic primary.

MARCH 30: Johnson announced he would not run for reelection.

APRIL 4: Martin Luther King, Jr. was assassinated. Rioters rampaged in over one hundred cities.

MAY 12–JUNE 30: Protesters marched against racism and poverty in Washington, DC.

JUNE 4–5: Presidential candidate Robert F. Kennedy won the California primary—and was assassinated.

AUGUST 8: The Republican National Convention nominated the conservative Richard Milhous Nixon as its presidential candidate.

AUGUST 28: Police attacked demonstrators at the Democratic National Convention.

NOVEMBER 5: Nixon won the presidency with only 43 percent of the popular vote.

When Hillary learned on April 4 that Dr. King had been murdered, she ran to her room and hurled her book bag against the wall. Shaking, she cried, "I can't stand it anymore! I can't take it!"[62]

King had been working for nonviolent change. She had grasped his hand, watched him describe his dream. And he was shot dead. She called her friend Karen to share her grief and condolences. The next day, Hillary and other members of WAR joined a massive march of protesters and mourners in Boston.

"I returned to campus," she said, "wearing a black armband and agonizing about the kind of future America faced."[63]

Some colleges held memorial services or cancelled classes in Dr. King's honor. Wellesley did not. Frustrated, black students demanded that the college increase the number of black students and faculty. They even threatened to go on a hunger strike unless the administration complied.

In her deft way of working with both sides, Hillary negotiated a compromise. Students agreed not to starve. The college agreed to start, eventually, a black studies program. At Hillary's urging, the school also hosted a summer tutorial for inner-city children. She helped everyone find the middle ground.

Now 100 percent against the war and leaning toward

declaring herself a Democrat, Hillary had been driving up to New Hampshire to work on Eugene McCarthy's primary campaign. With McCarthy's surprising showing in the primary and King's horrifying assassination, she ratcheted up her involvement in national affairs. When a high school friend wrote that he had decided to remain an "observer,"[64] Hillary shot back a retort asking how anyone could prefer to react than act. This was a lesson she had absorbed from her mother.

On the morning of June 5, 1968, her mother woke Hillary, who was back home briefly before moving to Washington, DC, for the summer. Robert Kennedy had been shot. Reeling, Hillary wondered "whether political action is worth the pain and struggle."[65] She would face that quandary again and again.

In high school, Mr. Carlson had assigned Hillary the Republican to take the role of the Democratic President Johnson. Now, Professor Schechter arranged for Hillary the Maybe Democrat to work for the House Republican Conference, which is composed of the Republican members of the House of Representatives. She objected, as she had in high school, but again to no avail. Her father, however, happily hung a photo of her with her bosses on his bedroom wall.

Hillary argued repeatedly with these congressmen—they were all men—about the war, which they supported. Nevertheless, they admired her spunk and diligence and invited her to attend the Republican National Convention in Miami. Excited to witness the presidential selection process up close, she accepted. She got to stay in a fancy hotel and order breakfast from room service.

More important, this was her chance to help a moderate candidate, New York's Governor Nelson Rockefeller, win the nomination. In favor of social causes like civil rights, he was her kind of heart-liberal Republican. She answered the telephone and opened mail in the Rockefeller hotel suite, just as she'd suggested to Brooke's supporters two years earlier.

The convention delegates, however, overwhelmingly voted for former Vice President Nixon, a sterner man. That act clinched her identity as a Democrat.

"I sometimes think that I didn't leave the Republican Party," she said, "as much as it left me."[66] It turned right (conservative). She turned left (liberal).

Back in Chicago at the end of the summer, Hillary and her school chum Betsy decided to head downtown, where the Democratic Convention was being held. Antiwar activists had called for mass demonstrations, and thousands of people from around the country poured into the city. Chicago's Mayor Richard Daley called out police, National Guardsmen, and soldiers, who attacked the protesters with clubs, fists, guns, and tear gas.

"Someone . . . threw a rock, which just missed us," Hillary said. "Betsy and I scrambled to get away as the police charged the crowd with nightsticks."[67] Shocked, they watched kids their age getting beaten in the head. The free-for-all continued for days.

There was talk that summer of revolution, of angry citizens overthrowing the government, like in 1776. But Hillary believed that political action, not warfare, "was the only route in a democracy for peaceful and lasting change."[68]

There are different kinds of actions, though. In just the past six months, she'd participated in elections, demonstrations, speeches, negotiations, organizing, and persuasion. What was the best way to ensure civil rights, end poverty, and improve education? Should people go to court? Change the law? Get elected to office? Protest?

Before she returned to college for her senior year, Hillary talked with a man she had met through Reverend Jones. Known as a "professional agitator," Saul Alinsky believed in getting "power to the people." For her senior honors thesis, Hillary studied his techniques and concluded that demonstrations aren't as effective as programs funded by the federal government. Still a mind-conservative, though, she worried that people might become dependent on such programs—on the government's dime—rather than stand on their own two feet. Finding the Goldilocks, just-right size for government programs haunted her years later.

Hillary decided she could do the most good by becoming a lawyer, rather than a protester. "You can't just take to the streets and make change in America,"[69] she reasoned. Instead, "the law can be an incredible vehicle for social change—and lawyers are at the wheel."[70]

In his letter of recommendation, Schechter wrote,

"She is by far the most outstanding young woman I have taught in the last seven years . . . She has the intellectual ability, personality, and character to make a remarkable contribution to American society."[71]

A professor at Harvard Law School must not have read the letter. When a student there told him that Hillary had been accepted at both Harvard and Yale, he peered down at her and said, "We don't need any more women."[72] Hillary picked Yale.

Looking back at that tumultuous period, Hillary called 1968 a "watershed year for the country, and for my own personal and political evolution."[73]

Commencement

Yellow and purple pitcher plants, weeping cherry trees, and lavender beardtongue blossomed across the Wellesley campus in May. Hillary and her classmates were hardly feeling serene, however, in the spring of 1969. They had been battling President Adams for months.

The young women had decided that, in addition to the official commencement speaker, a student should deliver a speech at their graduation—a peer who could convey what was in their hearts and minds. But Adams refused. As head of the college government, Hillary went to talk with her.

"What is the real objection?" Hillary asked.

"It's never been done," Adams responded.

Hillary hardly considered that an adequate reason. "We could give it a try," she nudged.

When Adams complained that she didn't know who the speaker would be, Hillary answered, "Well, they asked me." Eventually, the stodgy president gave in.

Hillary, however, didn't know what to say. So, just as she had when she ran for president of student government, she solicited ideas from her classmates. They slipped her notes and poems, jokes, and recollections.

"I spent hours talking to people about what they wanted me to say and hours more making sense of the disparate and conflicting advice I received,"[74] Hillary said.

Hugh and Dorothy hadn't planned to attend graduation. But, when she told them she was going to speak, her father made a last-minute trip, arriving late the night before. Her mother couldn't come because of health problems.

On graduation day, May 31, Hillary hurriedly rolled her hair into a bun, leaving straggling ends to dangle by her ears. The 401 members of the Class of '69, in caps and gowns, sat in rows on the lawn between the library and the chapel. Hillary joined President Adams and the official speaker, Senator Edward Brooke, on the dais. If she had seen the title of his presentation, "Real Problems and Wrong Procedures," she might have gotten a clue to his message.

"The waves of protests passing over the United States . . . create deep social tension,"[75] he stated. Demonstrations aren't solving problems; they are making them worse, he argued.

Hillary bristled. She had helped elect Brooke, and he was condemning the tactics of her generation.

Unaware of what Hillary was about to say, President Adams introduced her as "cheerful, good-humored, good company, and a good friend to all of us."[76]

Not at all cheerful, Hillary said she faced the "task of criticizing and constructive protest and I find myself reacting just briefly to some of the things that Senator

Brooke said."[77] She then publicly scolded a United States senator. "We protested against the rigid academic distribution requirement," she pointed out. "We have made progress." Furthermore, she explained, "Every protest, every dissent . . . is unabashedly an attempt to forge an identity."[78] This was the task she had assigned herself freshman year. Protests helped her and her class define themselves.

Implying that Brooke had failed as a politician, she asserted, "for too long, our leaders have viewed politics as the art of the possible."[79] Then she added, "the challenge now is to practice politics as the art of making what appears to be impossible, possible."[80]

The Class of '69 rose and gave her a seven-minute standing ovation. Once again, a classmate predicted, "She will probably be the president of the United States someday."[81]

Hillary's father seemed indifferent to her speech. Another father in the audience, however, huffed, "What a disrespectful young lady."[82] Senator Brooke, too, was incensed by her audacity.

Defying college rules, Hillary later stripped off her clothes and jumped into Lake Waban. President

Adams ordered a campus guard to confiscate them. Hillary concluded that Adams "was sorry she had ever let me speak."[83]

The *Boston Globe* ran a story the next day headlined, "Senator Brooke Upstaged at Wellesley Commencement."[84] *Life* magazine flew a crew to Chicago to interview and photograph her at home. Hillary Rodham, age twenty-one, was already famous.

Reflecting on her previous four years, Hillary reminisced, "Wellesley was a girls' school when we started and a women's college when we left. That sentiment probably said as much about us as it did the college. I arrived at Wellesley carrying my father's political beliefs . . . and left with the beginning of my own."[85]

. . . .

SUMMER OF '69

Just after graduation, Hillary served as maid of honor at the wedding of her good friend Jinnet Fowles. Jinnet, who had majored in art history, craved a modern sculpture that she'd seen in the college's art museum composed of a crushed car radiator. So, Hillary persuaded an automobile wrecking company to smash a radiator, which she proudly gave Jinnet for a wedding present.

Hillary then spent part of the summer sliming salmon on a pier in Alaska—until she was fired for complaining about the poor quality of both the fish and the working conditions.

. . . .

CHAPTER 3

*East Coast School, Southern Boy: Yale Law
School and Bill Clinton
1969–1974*

· ·

"She Was the Go-Between"

Seeing the brick spires and vaulted doorways of Yale
Law School, Hillary might have thought the place
would be similar to Wellesley. But Yale sits in New
Haven, Connecticut, a gritty urban center with a
notoriously high crime rate. Since her father stopped
paying her tuition after she graduated from Wellesley,
she had to support herself on a scholarship and student loans in the fall of 1969. No longer provided a
cozy dorm room, Hillary unstrapped her mattress,
which she'd hauled on top of her car, and moved into

a high-rise apartment building downtown.

Her new classmates also differed from those at Wellesley, in an important way. Out of 235 law students, only twenty-seven—barely more than 10 percent—were women. "This seems like a paltry number now," Hillary later said, "but it was a breakthrough at the time."[86]

Few women in those days entered professional schools, such as law or medicine; far more went into teaching or worked as secretaries. Only 3 percent of all the lawyers in the country were women. Occasionally, a Yale professor announced, "It's Ladies' Day!"[87] and called on just the women.

Hillary quickly noticed yet another difference from the quiet college atmosphere she'd recently left. Yalies filled the quadrangle lawn with tents, tables, and loudspeakers and held raucous teach-ins on the War in Vietnam and civil rights. Hillary had organized a teach-in at Wellesley but hardly anyone showed up; she had grumbled about the "large gray mass"[88] of uninterested students. At Yale, on the other hand, protests carried on for weeks.

Hillary reveled in the constant debates about justice and fairness in class and at local pizza hangouts.

Because of the article in *Life* magazine, professors and students recognized and listened to her.

In the spring of her first year, however, disputes on campus became bitter, and potentially violent. Members of the revolutionary Black Panther Party were being tried for murder in a federal courthouse in New Haven, and many students feared that the judge and jury would not give them a fair trial. They were further outraged when President Richard Nixon announced on April 30, 1970, that he was extending the war into another Southeast Asian country, Cambodia. Hillary called it an "expansion of a war that never should have been waged."[89]

Dejected, she wondered "what was to become of our school and our country." A professor urged her, "You cannot be discouraged. You have to keep trying."[90] She knew he was right, and in any case, she wasn't a quitter.

Students called a meeting to plan protests against the war, but the gathering turned rowdy. One faction clamored to strike, another to hold a sit-in at the dean's office. Although she was merely a first-year student, Hillary strode to the front of the room and perched on a table. Taking charge of the meeting, she listened to both sides and calmly summarized their arguments.

"She was the go-between,"[91] said Kris Olson, her college friend who was also at Yale Law. She continued to seek the middle ground.

Just as she had in '68, Hillary chose to act within the law rather than revolt. So did the other students, who voted to protest peacefully. Outside the courtroom on May 1, Hillary helped patrol a crowd of fifteen thousand demonstrators.

Some campuses weren't so fortunate. Three days later, National Guardsmen, ordered by the governor of Ohio to quell antiwar protests at Kent State University, killed four undergraduates. Hillary cried and later said, "It seemed at times that our government was at war with its own people."[92] Just as she had when Dr. King was assassinated, she wore a black armband in mourning.

"I Wanted to Give Voice to Children"

Hillary was still wearing the armband on May 7, 1970, when she gave a talk at a convention honoring the fiftieth anniversary of the League of Women Voters in Washington, DC. With anguish in her voice, she pleaded with these politically active older women to "help stop the chain of broken promises."[93] Help make America more equal for her generation.

The main speaker at the convention was a black woman named Marian Wright Edelman, who was about to become Hillary's boss and mentor. Hillary had made a point of meeting Marian the previous fall, after reading an article about her work on behalf of children. As a graduate of Yale Law School seven years earlier, Marian had decided to focus on the needs and rights of children. "Children," she believed, "are the unrecognized, neglected, and mistreated minority in America."[94]

This message resonated with Hillary. She remembered seven-year-old Maria, who lived in the migrant trailer camp. The youngsters she'd tutored in Boston who had fallen behind in school. Her college thesis on programs for poor people.

"Meeting . . . Marian, who had a passion about helping children and had a lot of the same values that I had, was a turning point in my life,"[95] Hillary said. She asked Marian if she could work for her that summer.

Marian was delighted to add a bright activist to her staff. But her small nonprofit organization, the Washington Research Project, had no money to pay her. So Hillary scrounged funds from a program at the law school that supported students eager to work on civil rights. In the summer of 1970, she set off for Washington, DC, the center of American politics.

Marian assigned Hillary to attend hearings held by Minnesota's Senator Walter Mondale. He had asked doctors to investigate the living conditions of migrant farm workers, like Maria. Hillary learned that families were housed in tiny cinder-block sheds without bathrooms or lighting; that children went deaf from untreated ear infections; that babies died from poor nutrition.

By the end of the summer, Hillary realized she wanted to "give voice to children who were not being heard."[96] She came back to school so "fired up,"[97] she dropped the usual second-year law classes. Instead, she studied how laws affect children. She worked at a medical center and proposed ways that hospitals could help children who had been abused and abandoned, like her mother. And, through volunteering for Legal Services, which gave legal advice to poor people, she tried to help a foster mother adopt a girl the mother had cared for since birth.

Hillary wrote an article arguing that children are citizens, just like adults. This was a new idea. Courts tended to treat children as the property of their parents, ignoring youngsters' needs and preferences. Hillary proposed ways to decide when the government had the right—the obligation, even—to remove kids from their parents.

Because Hillary didn't follow the law school curriculum, she had to spend an extra year in New Haven. But that turned out to be handy when she met—and soon fell in love with—a fellow student.

"She Was in My Face"

Six feet two inches tall, with a "reddish-brown beard and curly mane of hair,"[98] Bill Clinton looked more like a Viking, Hillary thought, than a lawyer-to-be. The first time she glimpsed him, he was boasting to other students that his home state of Arkansas grew the world's biggest watermelons. Later she learned that he'd followed her around campus for a semester, without getting up the nerve to talk to her. Finally, one night in the library in the spring of 1971, she noticed him staring at her, so she walked over to him.

"If you're going to keep looking at me," she said, "and I'm going to keep looking back, we might as well be introduced. I'm Hillary Rodham."[99] Most young women were not so forward. Bill was speechless, probably for the first time in his life. Later, he said, "She was in my face from the start, and, before I knew it, in my heart."[100]

They studied, practiced yoga, and traveled together, and, the whole time, they talked—and argued—about politics. By Christmas, Hillary decided to introduce Bill to her parents. When he arrived at her house in Park Ridge, Dorothy answered the door.

"Hello, my name is Bill Clinton," he said.

"That's nice," Dorothy replied, sounding like she wanted to block the doorway. She explained later, "I would have preferred that he left. He had come to take my daughter away!"[101]

Dorothy was especially chilly when she learned that Bill intended to return to Arkansas after law school to run for office. She had hoped Hillary would be appointed the first female Supreme Court justice and didn't think that would happen in what she assumed was a backward state. Hugh, who found Bill's accent strange, was even gruffer than Dorothy—until Bill sat down and watched football games on television with him.

Back at school in the spring of 1972, Hillary and Bill partnered in a mock trial competition, called a moot court, in front of a judge and jury. The trial case they wrote was based on a classic movie, which Hillary dramatized with costumes. She persuaded Kris to appear as a floozy character in a pair of fur shorts. As a lead attorney, Hillary wore a vivid orange dress to draw the jury's attention to herself. With his charming southern drawl and her legal expertise and sense of humor, they were sure to be a winning pair. Nevertheless, their team lost.

Kris recalled other fun times in law school. "She was really into the music of the time,"[102] she said. But everyone agreed that Hillary had what Wellesley classmate Nancy Gist called "the worst singing voice EVER!"[103] So, she lip-synched to records of popular groups, holding a vacuum-cleaner hose as a fake microphone.

During the summer of 1972, Hillary again worked for Marian. She investigated segregated schools in Alabama by pretending to be a mother looking for a school for her child. She was appalled when principals assured her that "no black students would be enrolled"[104] with her pretend white child.

"Fearless"

Meanwhile, Bill moved to Austin, Texas, to help organize that state's presidential campaign for Senator George McGovern. An antiwar candidate from South Dakota, McGovern was running against the incumbent, President Richard Nixon. Bill asked Hillary to join him. But she was torn and shared her concerns with a friend. Should she follow her own career path and give voice to children by working with Marian? Or should she follow Bill?

"Power struggles were real," her friend recalled. "Feminism was in a strident moment."[105] "Feminism"—the belief that women and men are equal and should have the same legal rights—was a newly popular word, and people were figuring out what it meant in everyday life. Many of Hillary's college friends were active in NOW, lobbying state legislatures to pass the Equal Rights Amendment, and demanding day care for their children so they could go to work.

. . . .

THE EQUAL RIGHTS AMENDMENT

In the early twentieth century, activists for women's rights believed that the best way to ban discrimination against women was to add an amendment to the Constitution. This process requires two steps. First, two-thirds of the members of both the House and the Senate must support the amendment. Then, three-quarters of the state legislatures must agree to it.

Alice Paul, the founder of the National Women's Party, introduced the Equal Rights Amendment (ERA) in 1923. Little happened until the House approved it in 1970; the Senate did so in 1972. Within a year, thirty state legislatures ratified—passed—the amendment. But eight more states were needed.

Opponents, including some women, argued that, if the ERA passed, women would be drafted, and they organized to defeat it. The process ended in 1982, with three states still needed. Supporters were deeply disappointed that legal equality between men and women was not made part of the Constitution.

. . . .

Hillary decided that she couldn't just traipse after Bill. If she was going to Texas, she needed a job of her own. When a campaign organizer there offered her one near the end of the summer of '72, she "jumped at the chance."[106]

The Twenty-Sixth Amendment to the Constitution had passed the previous summer, giving eighteen-year-olds the right to vote. Many people believed, as Hillary had said at a conference, "If young people were old enough to fight, they were entitled to vote."[107] Although Texans had voted for Democrats in the past, polls predicted that McGovern would lose there. Campaign workers hoped that, if enough young people voted, they could tip the election. So Hillary and some locals drove around South Texas, urging them to register.

"Hispanics . . . were, understandably, wary of a blond girl from Chicago who didn't speak a word of

Spanish,"[108] she said. Especially one who looked like an East Coast geek in thick glasses, no makeup, and clunky shoes.

She might have been wary, too, of some of the tough neighborhoods she visited. But she remained "Fearless," as a colleague nicknamed her. Hillary ate *menudo* (soup made from cow stomach), let loose with her raucous laugh, and got along well with everyone. Many of them approved when they saw her read and make notes in the Bible she carried around.

"Texans loved her," said a local man who was active in state politics. "She was perfect!"[109]

Betsey Wright, a campaign organizer, was so impressed with Hillary's energy and brilliance that she encouraged her to run for office. "I was obsessed with how far Hillary might go," Betsey said, anticipating "the incredible things she could do in the world."[110]

Rather than return to Yale for the fall semester of their final year in law school, Hillary and Bill played hooky to work for McGovern until Election Day. But near the end of October, they dashed out of the campaign office in Austin and stopped one of their coworkers who had a car. "Take us to the airport," she insisted.

"We've got to go to Yale to register late for law school. This is the last day!"[111]

Not only had Hillary and Bill not attended classes all fall, they hadn't even signed up for any. They hurriedly chose courses, registered, and flew back to Texas. Bill had to organize poll workers. Hillary had to staff the headquarters in San Antonio. They worked eighteen-hour days.

Nevertheless, only one-third of Texas's voters supported McGovern. Nationwide, he won in only one state and the District of Columbia. Nixon was reelected in a landslide.

This was the pair's first joint political effort, and Hillary realized, "We still had much to learn about the art of political campaigning."[112] She and Bill discussed how to raise money, how to use television (social media didn't exist then), and how hard it is to win.

They returned to school in time for exams, which they aced. After graduating from law school in spring 1973, they took a trip to England. Bill wanted to show Hillary where he'd gone to graduate school, at the University of Oxford, on a prestigious Rhodes Scholarship.

One evening, he asked her to marry him. She didn't

exactly reject him. She simply said, "Not now." This was the first of his many proposals.

Knowing the pain that her grandparents' divorce had caused her mother, she needed time to be sure that she could commit to Bill forever. "I thought of him as a force of nature and wondered whether I'd be up to the task of living through his seasons,"[113] she explained. Furthermore, she knew that he planned to return to Arkansas. "I wanted nothing to do with that,"[114] she admitted.

She agreed, however, to meet Bill's mother in Hot Springs. Hillary, in blue jeans and a work shirt, and Virginia, in false eyelashes and white-striped hair, stared at each other.

"Bill, she's so *different*,"[115] Virginia exclaimed.

"We were each bewildered,"[116] Hillary said.

Nevertheless, Bill pleaded with his mother. "I want you to pray for me that it's Hillary because if it isn't Hillary, it's nobody."[117]

"She Wanted to Go to School . . ."

"Americans think of themselves as a child-loving people. This is a myth."[118]

This is the first line of a report, titled *Children Out of School in America*, that Hillary worked on after law school. She'd accepted a job with Marian, who had evolved the Washington Research Project into the Children's Defense Fund (CDF). As a member of a team of researchers and lawyers, Hillary interviewed children who had been excluded from school. They were either not admitted or had been kicked out because they were too poor to pay for books, didn't speak English, had physical disabilities, or were in jail—often, she discovered, with adult prisoners.

"I met a girl in a wheelchair," Hillary said, "who told me how much she wanted to go to school. She knew she couldn't go because she couldn't walk."[119] Hillary was determined to help her and other kids like her.

As a result of this report and efforts by many other groups, Congress passed a law two years later requiring public schools to teach children with disabilities. Hillary was proud of her contributions. But, after several months with CDF, another opportunity arose, and again she jumped at the chance, grabbing the next ring on the playground crossbars.

"A System That Truly Does Work"

While Hillary was working in Texas the previous year, a series of odd news stories caught everyone's attention. First, five men broke into the Democratic National Headquarters at the Watergate office complex in Washington, DC. Next, connections were discovered between these burglars and the Republican campaign to reelect President Nixon. Journalists with the *Washington Post* investigated and reported on these mysterious events.

By the end of 1973, there was strong evidence that the president might have ordered the break-in and then lied about it. He could be impeached for these crimes. Nixon defended himself by exclaiming, "I'm not a crook!"[120] But people suspected he lied about that, too.

The Judiciary Committee of the House of Representatives voted to investigate the apparent crimes and decide whether or not to proceed with impeaching the president. The committee hired a man named John Doar to serve as special prosecutor and investigate Nixon. Doar had judged the competition Bill and Hillary had entered at Yale. He called Bill, who was teaching at the University of Arkansas School of Law in Fayetteville, and asked him to join his staff.

. . . .

IMPEACHMENT OF THE PRESIDENT

The impeachment process begins when the Judiciary Committee of the House of Representatives holds hearings to investigate whether the president has committed "high crimes or misdemeanors." These crimes are described in Article II, Section 4 of the US Constitution. (Other officers, besides the president, can also be impeached.) If a majority of the members of the House present formal charges against the president, he or she is tried by the Senate. If two-thirds of the Senate vote to convict, the president is removed from office. Two presidents have been impeached—Andrew Johnson in 1868, and Bill Clinton. Neither was removed from office.

. . . .

Bill responded that he couldn't help because he was considering running for Congress. Instead, he recommended Hillary for the coveted job. Doar agreed. She joined the staff to investigate the president in January

1974. She was just twenty-six years old and one of only three female lawyers out of a total of forty-four.

The working conditions, in a former hotel in Washington, were grim. Bathrooms were turned into offices. Prison-like bars covered the windows. Doors clanged with heavy steel locks. Doar insisted on absolute secrecy. Staff could not keep diaries, talk to anyone else about their work, or even go to parties. Anyway, they didn't have time, since they shut themselves in their offices for twelve to eighteen hours, seven days a week.

Late one night, Hillary told her supervisor, Bernard Nussbaum, that her boyfriend was coming from Arkansas to visit the next day.

"Bernie," she said, "he's going to be president of the United States."

Exhausted from the heavy workload, he yelled, "Hillary, that's the most idiotic—I'm working with a bunch of idiots!"

"You don't know a thing you're talking about,"[121] she shouted back, and stalked off. The next day, they apologized to each other.

Frustrated by some of the men's assumptions about who should do what work, Hillary helped post a sign in the break room. It read, "The women in this office were not hired to make coffee. Make it yourself . . ."[122] That was part of what feminism meant in everyday life.

Hillary had three major responsibilities:

- Analyze the chain of command in Nixon's White House, to figure out what decisions the president might have made.
- Draft procedures for the Judiciary Committee to follow.
- Determine the definitions and examples of "high crimes and misdemeanors" for which a president could be impeached. Hillary argued for a broad definition, which later came to haunt her.

Nixon had audiotaped conversations he held with staff in the Oval Office. He also taped himself "explaining" what he'd meant while he was covering up his crimes. Wearing large headphones and locked in a soundproof room, Hillary listened to many of the recordings.

Because he expanded the war in Vietnam and Cambodia, she had once called Nixon "evil"[123] and believed he deserved to be impeached. Nevertheless, Doar insisted, she said, "that no one draw conclusions until all the facts were evaluated."[124] Each fact that every staffer uncovered was typed onto a separate index card. By the end, they had compiled over half a million cards. Only a few people knew the whole story. One of them was Hillary.

On July 19, 1974, after six and a half months of intense labor, Doar proposed articles of impeachment; that is, accusations against the president. Based on the clear and careful evidence, the Judiciary Committee approved three articles. Three weeks later, the White House released a tape on which the public heard Nixon agreeing to pay the burglars to cover up the Watergate break-in.

Surely, the Senate would convict him and force him from office, Hillary believed. Instead, on August 9, President Nixon resigned.

Hillary had several reactions. Her faith in government was renewed. She said, "We have a system that truly does work, if only we become involved in it."[125] On the other hand, she realized, "Suddenly I was out of work."[126]

Hillary had many options. With her experience, she could get a job with a law firm or return to the

Children's Defense Fund. She also received an offer to teach at the University of Arkansas School of Law alongside Bill, who was committed to staying in the state. Hillary asked a female colleague from Arkansas what it was like there.

"Tough. Very tough," she answered. "You just had to prove yourself three hundred percent."[127]

Yet, in the end, Hillary realized, "I had no choice but to follow my heart."[128]

CHAPTER 4

Arkansas?!
1974–1992

· ·

"Sou-ee, Pig!"

"Are you out of your mind?"[129]

Sara Ehrman, a friend Hillary had stayed with in Washington, asked her that question repeatedly. It was late summer 1974, and they were driving 1,200 miles to Fayetteville, Arkansas, deep in the Ozark Mountains.

"You're going to this rural, remote place—and you'll wind up married to some country lawyer,"[130] Sara warned.

Hillary loved and admired Bill, so she knew Sara's fears were exaggerated. Yet she also knew that Arkansas had a long history of racism and a reputation for being backward. The state was almost the poorest in the country, and many houses, roads, and stores looked ramshackle.

Every few miles of the drive, Sara asked Hillary if she knew what she was doing. "No, but I'm going anyway,"[131] Hillary insisted. Sara slowed down and took detours, hoping her friend would change her mind. They reached sweltering Fayetteville just in time for a rally for the university's football team, the Razorbacks.

"Everybody in town was wearing . . . pig hats and screaming," Sara said. "*Sou-ee, sou-ee, pig, pig, pig.* I was just appalled."[132]

However, after hearing Bill speak at a campaign event that night, both women realized Hillary had been right. Bill Clinton was going to be a successful politician and help his state. Maybe even the country.

In any case, Hillary believed you should "bloom where you're planted."[133] She'd just have to bloom in pig country.

"They Had Better Ideas"

Just as at Wellesley, Hillary had a heavy course load at the university. But now, she was the professor. She taught criminal law, trial work, and clinics on prisons and legal aid. The clinics, like Legal Services, both provided advice to poor people and trained students. She and her students handled three hundred cases that year.

A fellow faculty member, Steve Nickles, often saw Hillary leaning against a wall in the hallway, talking with her students. "She took that job seriously," he said. "She was concerned about . . . the law and how it affected people . . . She was constantly mentoring students."[134]

"She made you think, she challenged you,"[135] a student said. And her final exams were tough.

Local judges, however, were less pleased with the "new lady law professor."[136] One refused to hear her cases, saying, "I have no use for legal aid."[137] Like her father, the judge didn't want to help poor people. Hillary admitted, "I wondered what on earth I'd gotten myself into."[138]

Fayetteville turned out to be a quirky college town, though, where, pretty soon, even the grocery store clerks and telephone operators seemed to know her whereabouts.

"I had never before lived in a place so small, friendly and Southern," Hillary said, "and I loved it."[139]

Hillary lived in a modern stone, timber, and glass house on Pig Trail, situated on eighty acres of pasture-land bordered by a river. While most people in the state "called the hogs" at weekend football games, she invited her colleagues over to play volleyball and charades and, of course, discuss politics. They didn't just talk about who might win the next election. Hillary and Bill wanted to solve big problems, like how the government could improve local schools and support families.

"They had better ideas,"[140] Steve said. They wanted to know not only why people's welfare checks arrived late—a common complaint—but also why so many Arkansans needed welfare. Maybe the whole welfare system needed to be reformed.

Hillary also helped Bill plan his campaign. To her delight, her Republican father and brother came down from Chicago as "official sign putter-uppers." Local campaigners, though, didn't feel Hillary was much help. She didn't know Arkansas the way they did, and one complained that she "managed to antagonize the entire staff."[141]

Hillary was accustomed to finding the middle ground, as she had in college and law school. But here, it seemed that she occasionally lost her footing.

And Bill lost his race. As they had in Texas, the pair debated their strategy, sometimes hotly, to figure out how to do better in case he ran again. Hillary also considered leaving—leaving Bill, his political ambitions, the state. She traveled back to Chicago, Boston, and Washington to talk with old friends and ponder her future. Again, she realized, "I love him."[142] She returned to Arkansas.

Bill picked her up at the tiny Fayetteville airport and drove past a little house she had admired several months earlier. Built with "clinker" (bumpy) bricks and a steeply pitched, cross-gabled roof, it looked like a fairy-tale cottage.

"I bought it," Bill told her, "so now you'd better marry me because I can't live in it by myself."[143] This time, she accepted his proposal.

On October 11, 1975, Hillary Diane Rodham and William Jefferson Clinton were married in the house at 930 California Boulevard. Several days earlier, she'd called a few friends to invite them to the wedding. A Wellesley roommate took the bus; Betsy came down from Chicago. When her mother discovered the night before that Hillary had not bought a gown, they took a break from repainting the house—yellow, Hillary's favorite color, in the dining room—and dashed to the mall.

Hillary found a high-necked, poufy-sleeved Victorian dress made of muslin and lace. "This will be fine,"[144] she said. She still didn't care about clothes—not even for her own wedding.

During the ceremony, the minister had to urge Hugh to let Hillary go when he asked, "Who will give away this woman?"[145] Afterward, friends held a reception where two hundred guests served themselves from a champagne fountain. Two months later, the happy couple took a honeymoon trip to Acapulco, Mexico—along with her entire family.

Steve said about their marriage, "There was a very strong partnership. Each fueled the other."[146] They maintained the partnership, though there would be times when the fuel burst into flames.

"Keeping My Professional Life Separate"

Two elections in 1976 steered Hillary's life in new directions. Governor Jimmy Carter of Georgia ran for president, and Bill Clinton ran for attorney general of Arkansas. Both candidates won.

Carter asked Hillary to help run his campaign in Indiana. Although there was no chance he'd win the electoral college vote in this hard-core Republican state, she agreed to spend several months there rallying as many citizens as possible to vote for him. As she had in Texas, she learned practical election skills, like how to budget and how to get voters to the polls. These experiences would come in handy if Bill kept running for office.

Bill's victory meant that Hillary would have to give up her teaching job and move to Little Rock, a larger but less open-minded town than Fayetteville. More important, she was about to become a politician's wife.

Hillary talked with a friend in Fayetteville, Ann

Henry, whose husband was a member of the state legislature. Ann warned her that she wouldn't be able to have a full-time career of her own or even say whatever she thought any longer. Politicians are so busy and are followed so closely by the press, Ann explained, that their spouses cannot have private, independent lives.

Hillary got an inkling of this predicament when a reporter asked her husband if he thought that her using her maiden name, Rodham, would hurt his chances.

All Bill could say was, "I hope not."[147]

Most women adopted their husband's last name, especially in conservative states like Arkansas, which valued traditional family life. But for Hillary, retaining Rodham "seemed like a sensible way of keeping my professional life separate from [Bill's] political life,"[148] she explained. "While I was committed to our union, I was still me."[149]

Disagreeing with Ann—and needing a salary to supplement Bill's small income—she accepted a job with the Rose Law Firm, Little Rock's most prominent group of lawyers. Hillary was its first female attorney.

She discovered that the men got together after work for drinks and on the weekends for golf. She wanted to socialize but also to behave properly. A married woman was not supposed to be seen in the company of another man. Nor was a married man supposed to keep company with any woman other than his wife. Instead of meeting after hours, Hillary had lunch many days with two close colleagues, Vincent Foster and Webster Hubbell. Still, people gossiped. She wondered if Ann had a point, after all. As an independent woman, she felt more out of place here than in Fayetteville.

At Rose, Hillary found herself defending large corporations and criminals instead of poor people. In her first jury trial, she represented a canning company against a man who'd sued after he discovered the rear end of a rat in his can of pork and beans! She knew that everyone, even a company accused of making disgusting mistakes, deserves a day in court.

Hillary also continued her work on behalf of foster children. Unlike in New Haven, this time, she won her case. As a result, a two-year-old was allowed to stay with the family the toddler had known since birth. In addition, Hillary helped found the Arkansas Advocates for Children and Families, an organization that promotes the health and welfare of young people.

"Exhilarating, Glorious"

As a professor and a lawyer, Hillary remained mostly anonymous. When Bill decided to run for governor in 1978, however, people all over the state began to take notice of Hillary Rodham.

During the campaign, conservatives criticized her for keeping her name, practicing law, and fraternizing with married men. They also claimed that Bill was a "draft-dodger" who had avoided being sent to Vietnam. Both feminism and the war, matters that Hillary had started dealing with in college, remained issues for her. The couple was beginning to experience the nasty charges that political opponents fling at each other.

Nevertheless, Bill was popular, and he won the election with over 60 percent of the vote. At age thirty-two, he became one of the youngest governors in the nation's history. The new First Lady of Arkansas—"FLOAR"—was only thirty-one.

The governor's term was two years. Hillary said of that period, "The years 1978 through 1980 were among the most difficult, exhilarating, glorious, and heartbreaking in my life."[150]

They moved from their tiny house near downtown into an imposing mansion that was ten times larger in the historic Quapaw Quarter. Cooks, cleaners, drivers, and a security detail looked after them. Hillary had never lived anyplace so grand.

Professionally, she flourished. The Rose Firm promoted her to partner status—the first female partner, or officer, the firm had ever had. Both the Children's Defense Fund and the Legal Services Corporation (LSC) appointed her to their national boards of directors. Hoping to boost the family income, she invested in several ventures. One of them, called Whitewater, planned to build and sell vacation homes in the Ozarks.

Bill named his wife head of the state's new Rural Health Advisory Committee, which established health clinics and recruited nurses and midwives to poor rural areas. Because Hillary had helped elect President Carter and because Bill was an up-and-coming young Democrat, they were invited to dinners at the White House.

The couple was especially exhilarated when Hillary became pregnant. They'd been hoping for a baby since they married. They had chosen a name for a girl over a year earlier. While strolling through the Chelsea neighborhood of London, England, they, coincidentally, overheard a recording of a favorite folk song, "Chelsea Morning."

Bill suggested, "If we ever have a daughter, we should name her Chelsea."[151] Hillary agreed.

The other parents-to-be in their birthing class were surprised to see the governor practicing breathing techniques. A judge told Hillary he didn't believe husbands should be in the delivery room. Bill was present anyway when Chelsea Victoria Clinton was born on February 27, 1980, just hours after he returned from a White House dinner.

"When I had Chelsea, I was full of nerves," Hillary admitted. "Despite all the preparation, I was unprepared for the sheer miracle and responsibility of parenthood."[152] Both Dorothy and Virginia helped out, giving grandmotherly advice. Even Hugh got down on his hands and knees to play with the baby. "I couldn't believe how that gruff and imposing man just melted in the palm of his granddaughter,"[153] Hillary marveled.

She bonded with her crying infant, saying, "Chelsea,

this is new for both of us. I've never been a mother before, and you've never been a baby. We're just going to have to help each other do the best we can."[154] Hillary continues to share that calming advice with other first-time mothers.

"Difficult and Heartbreaking"

With these happy events, why was the period between 1978 and 1980 also "difficult . . . and heartbreaking"? To everyone's surprise—even that of the pollsters who asked citizens how they planned to vote—Bill lost his bid for reelection.

The campaign had been nasty again, with Bill's opponent charging that he didn't care about Arkansans. There was also the issue of Hillary's last name. Ann told her that guests were offended to receive invitations to the mansion from "Governor Bill Clinton and Hillary Rodham."[155] It looked as if they weren't married—and they had a baby!

"Not using [the governor's] name," Steve said, "that's not good politics. That contributed to the view that she was too liberal for the state."[156] Hillary admitted that she learned her lesson "the hard way."[157]

The loss affected the family in many ways. The couple had to find a place to live as well as—like all working parents—babysitters, cars, and time to play with their child. Bill had to get a job and started work at a law firm. Feeling dejected by the outcome of the election and rejected by the voters, he sometimes stayed out late at night. Hillary wasn't sure where he went and wondered if her husband was spending time with other women. They argued and debated whether or not to stay together.

Hillary turned to her church for comfort. Her women's prayer group sent scripture readings, which she collected in a notebook and kept nearby with her Bible. She also traveled around the state, giving a talk titled "Why I Am a Methodist." Explaining John Wesley's command "that society do right by all its people"[158] strengthened her commitment to public service. She was determined to do whatever she could to help Bill return to office so they could put their big ideas to work for the good of Arkansas.

"It's Just Not That Big a Deal"

Looking back, Hillary realized, "as the First Lady of Arkansas, I was thrown into an unblinking spotlight. And for the first time, I came to realize how my personal choices could impact my husband's political future."[159] The spotlight kept growing brighter.

Over the next several years, Hillary changed her personal style. She lightened and poufed her hair and exchanged her heavy glasses for contact lenses, which had become easier to wear. Kris noticed that "Arkansas changed the way she dressed."[160] Other college friends even heard a new, Southern accent when she dropped her "g's" at the end of words. They barely recognized her. But Hillary knew she couldn't remain "an oddity,"[161] as if she didn't belong there.

On February 27, 1982, she gave Bill a present—a photograph of the three of them engraved "Chelsea's second birthday, Bill's second chance."[162] That day, he announced his campaign to take back the governor's seat. Hillary also took a leave from her job to help run his campaign. Most important, she started calling herself Hillary Rodham Clinton. She told Bill, "I couldn't bear it if this [her maiden name] cost you the election. It's just not that big a deal to me anymore."[163]

Hillary's identity did remain central to her, as it had since she was in college. But she was willing to find other ways to express it, particularly in her ongoing focus on children, women, and families.

Some people started referring to her as HRC. Her dearest friends thought of themselves as FOH (Friends of Hillary). His were FOB (Friends of Bill). Together, the couple became known as Billary.

With Chelsea, toys, and diaper bag in tow, they hit the campaign trail. In November 1982, Bill won with 55 percent of the vote. They returned to the governor's mansion and stayed for ten years.

· ·

HILLARY'S SERVICE AND HONORS IN ARKANSAS

During the eighteen years that Hillary lived in Arkansas, she served on and, in some cases, chaired sixteen boards of directors or commissions. In addition to the Children's Defense Fund and Legal Services Corporation, these included the American Bar Association

Commission on Women in the Profession, Wal-Mart Stores, the Southern Development Bancorporation, Child Care Action Campaign, Youth and America's Future, and a task force on infant mortality.

Hillary also received a dozen state and national honors, including Arkansas Woman of the Year in 1983 and Outstanding Layman of the Year for Contributions to Education in 1984. And she was cited as one of the Best Lawyers in America.

. . . .

"We Might Have Elected the Wrong Clinton!"

Hillary and Bill discussed Arkansas's greatest needs. They agreed that they had to grow the economy. To create jobs, they imported a banking system from Bangladesh, a country in Southeast Asia, which gave small loans to small businesses. To lure jobs from other places, Arkansas needed a better educational system. The state's Supreme Court had recently decided that the system's method of funding school districts was unfair. Poor areas were losing out, and Hillary wanted to make things right.

So in 1983, Bill established an Education Standards Committee to improve the schools. He appointed Hillary its chair. This was a risky political move. Hillary wasn't an educator. And she wasn't elected to office. *Why should the governor's wife have the power to overhaul the schools?* some critics wondered. Bill was insistent.

"I will have a person who is closer to me than anyone else overseeing a project that is more important to me than anything else,"[164] he argued.

Just as she had when she ran for head of college government at Wellesley, Hillary asked citizens for their opinions. She held hearings in each of the state's seventy-five counties. Over and over, the committee heard parents complain that teachers weren't prepared—some couldn't even read. As a result, the committee recommended that teachers as well as students meet certain standards. The rallying cry became "No more excuses!"[165]

Implementing the recommendations would be expensive. The legislature, which was notoriously penny-pinching, would have to raise taxes to pay for the new programs. Hillary testified before the state's House of Representatives to persuade them to pass a tax hike. She did such a good job that one member exclaimed, "Well, fellas, it looks like we might have elected the wrong Clinton!"[166]

The plan passed. But, in exchange, teachers had to take a test to keep their jobs.

"This enraged the teachers union," Hillary said. Teachers found the test insulting. A school librarian accused her of being "lower than a snake's belly."[167] On the other hand, many parents liked it. Hillary was described as being "polarizing;" that is, someone people either love or hate.

Hillary believed the new plan was a success for the school system. But she worried about the education of children not yet old enough to go to school. Traveling the state, she discovered that many parents did not read or talk to their young children. So, she imported a program from Israel called Home Instruction for Parents of Preschool Youngsters (HIPPY), which helps parents play with and teach their toddlers.

Chelsea

Meanwhile, Hillary was finding it both fun and challenging to raise her own child in the governor's mansion. As soon as they moved back, they had to replace the wrought-iron balustrade on the staircase. The railings were too far apart, and Chelsea could fall through.

Hillary made time for Chelsea in the morning and evening, before and after work. The two of them would lie on the rug in the grand entry hall and look at the colors that the crystal chandelier reflected onto the ceiling—just like Dorothy's lying on the grass and pointing out cloud shapes when Hillary was a little girl.

At bedtime, Chelsea snuggled in her mother's lap while Hillary sang "Moon River." That ended the night Chelsea realized that Hillary couldn't carry a tune, put her finger on her lips, and said, "No sing, Mommy, no sing."[168]

When she was old enough, Chelsea took piano lessons. After class one day, she reached toward a stray black-and-white kitten in her teacher's yard. The kitten jumped into Chelsea's arms. Socks moved into the mansion too.

Chelsea had other activities as well. Neighborhood friends came to the mansion's grounds to enjoy her outdoor playhouse. When Chelsea was in the first grade, Hillary and three other mothers taught science to the class because it wasn't part of the regular curriculum. Later, Chelsea attended a sleepaway foreign-language camp over the summers. Hillary reconnected with her college friend Jinnet, whose daughter attended the same camp. The two families drove together to drop off and pick up their children. Chelsea's favorite activity, though, was ballet, and her favorite production was *The Nutcracker.*

Hillary got together with other Wellesley classmates when she held a wedding reception at the mansion for their friend Jan Piercy. Many women stayed for the weekend, and one night, Hillary announced, "It's girls' night out!"[169] While they went out on the town in Little Rock, Bill babysat. Jinnet's son had no idea his babysitter was the governor of Arkansas!

"What Happens If We Win?"

Bill remained a popular governor and continued to win reelection. He also got attention on the national scene when he was made head of the National Governors Association. In 1987, Democrats asked him to run for president of the United States, just as Hillary had predicted.

The couple discussed the possibility. If he won, they could "do all the good" on a grand scale. A presidential race, however, would be costly and exhausting. They'd also be in a much brighter and larger spotlight—and so would their daughter.

To prepare Chelsea, who was six years old, for the rigors of a campaign, they told her about some of the mean things that political opponents might say about her parents. They held mock debates in which Hillary would state, "This Governor Clinton has done a terrible job." When Chelsea asked why anyone would say that, Bill answered, "I don't know, but we just want you to know it may happen."[170]

Realizing that a campaign would require him to travel for much of the next year, Bill decided not to run in 1988. He didn't want to leave his daughter for long periods.

When Chelsea was eleven, however, Hillary and Bill reconsidered. In the summer of 1991, they invited several close friends and advisors over for breakfast. Sitting around the kitchen table, they brainstormed who might run against him and debated his chances. Bill decided to run for the presidency. He would have to travel, but he promised Chelsea he'd come to her *Nutcracker* performance in December.

A friend asked, "What happens if we win?"

Hillary answered, "We'll change things."[171]

CHAPTER 5

The Media and the Journey to the
White House
1992–1993

● ●

"We Had to Manage Our Emotions"

Running for president is a team sport, like football or soccer. No one can do it alone. Fans cheer while opponents boo. Only one side wins. And the candidate often feels less like the team captain than like the ball—kicked around. In 1992, that's how Hillary and Bill felt, especially under the media's relentless glare.

As with any championship, Bill also had to win a series of preliminary games to get to the finals. First, he had to beat his rivals in the Democratic primary elections to earn the nomination. Then, after the nominating convention, he had to defeat not only his Republican rival, President George H. W. Bush, but also an independent candidate, Ross Perot.

Both men were prominent figures. As the current officeholder, Bush received free media attention because everything the president does is newsworthy. It's hard to beat a sitting president. Perot was a wealthy, outspoken businessman who could afford to pay for ads on television and travel around the country.

The national press didn't know the Clintons well. When journalists started looking into their lives, they found much that they liked, such as the couple's work on education, rural health care, roads, and other improvements in Arkansas.

On the other hand, the media were also very critical. Just because Bill had run his home state, which was small and poor, did not mean he could lead the United States. He knew hardly anything about America's relations with foreign countries.

The press also investigated the Clintons' personal lives and even mocked Hillary's headbands and hairdos. She was especially troubled when journalists asked the husband-and-wife team about their marriage. She believed that their disagreements with each other and rumors that he spent time with other women weren't anyone else's business.

Nevertheless, in January 1992, the pair decided to clear the air on-air, during a televised news program called *60 Minutes*. When the interviewer seemed to criticize their relationship, Hillary snapped, "I'm not sitting here, some little woman standing by my man like Tammy Wynette." She was referring to Wynette's country song urging women to stick by their man, no matter what. Hillary added, "I'm sitting here because I love him and I respect him."[172] That part of her message, however, got lost.

Tammy Wynette demanded—and received—an apology from Hillary, who regretted her outburst. Thousands of the singer's fans were furious. The interview had unnerved Hillary because the questions touched on matters that she felt should be private.

"We had to manage our emotions in the glare of the public spotlight,"[173] Hillary said. During much of the campaign, she did not manage hers very well and was at odds with the press.

Another reporter asked her whether Bill, as governor,

had steered legal business to her law firm in Little Rock. If she had gotten paid for legal advice that her firm gave to Bill, there could have been a conflict of interest, which would be a crime. The Rose Firm did do legal work for the state of Arkansas. But Hillary had made sure that she did not make money from it.

Hillary replied that women who are married to politicians and also have their own careers are looked at with suspicion. As an alternative to working, she said, "I suppose I could have stayed home and baked cookies and had teas, but what I decided to do was fulfill my profession."[174] Stay-at-home mothers, who do much more than bake cookies and hold teas, felt insulted. They too were furious.

"It wasn't my most eloquent moment,"[175] Hillary confessed. In just the first several months of the campaign, she had offended a large number of traditional women.

Hillary was not alone in making gaffes. Proud of her achievements, Bill joked to a crowd of supporters, "Buy one, get one free."[176] Vote for him, and get Hillary's skills too. The line went over well with some people. As a friend from their days working for McGovern said, "In Texas, we're used to strong women."[177]

But the remark backfired when opponents accused Hillary of wanting to be copresident rather than First Lady. After all, she wasn't the one running for office. Yet politicians and the press criticized her as if she were.

"We were unprepared for the hardball politics and relentless scrutiny that comes with a run for the Presidency,"[178] she said. Rival candidates had made nasty comments during statewide campaigns in Arkansas. But the national stage, Hillary was discovering, was downright "mean-spirited."[179]

Their enemies tripped them up by distorting their words. But Hillary and Bill tripped over themselves, as well.

Hillary responded to the attacks in several ways, including as a mom. She had sheltered Chelsea so successfully from the press that many Americans didn't know she and Bill had a child. So the three Clintons appeared, relaxed and smiling, on the cover of *People* magazine. Hillary also entered a mock cookie-baking contest against the wives of Bill's opponents—and won with a recipe for oatmeal chocolate-chip cookies.

She hopscotched around the country during the campaign, and her friend Jinnet caught up with her during a stop in Minneapolis. Jinnet posed a hypothetical dilemma. "If a good fairy dropped out of the sky and said, 'Well, Hillary, you get to choose. Does Chelsea get a role in *The Nutcracker*? Or does Bill get the Democratic nomination?'" Hillary replied, "I think I'd go for *The Nutcracker*."[180] Forced to choose, she'd rather see her daughter excel at her passion than have her husband run for president.

"Take Political Attacks Seriously but Not Personally"

Nevertheless, Hillary was in the election game to win, and she fought back against the challengers. Contending that no accusation should go unanswered, she created a war room, in which campaign strategists, including herself, planned counteroffensives. Recalling her sports-playing days, she said, "You have to learn how to take political attacks seriously but not personally."[181] Hillary might have also remembered the lesson she'd learned from Suzy, her neighbor in Chicago: hit back.

Throughout the early spring, Bill bounced up and

down in the polls. But by March 1992, he had won enough primary elections to win the Democratic Party's nomination for the presidency. The convention was held in July in New York City's Madison Square Garden. A consultant suggested that Chelsea stand alone, spotlighted on the stage in the darkened arena, and introduce her father to the 4,200 delegates. Hillary's reaction: "NO!"[182] She explained, "We signed up for this [politics] but Chelsea did not. She's a child. Leave her out of this."[183]

Chelsea did appear, however, holding her parents' hands, on the third night of the convention when her father received the official nomination. Silver confetti rained from the ceiling as a band played "The Stars and Stripes Forever" and a Fleetwood Mac song with the words "Don't stop thinking about tomorrow."

The campaign then went into high gear. Hillary and Bill took a bus tour of America with the vice presidential candidate, Senator Al Gore of Tennessee, and his wife, Tipper. An "excellent adventure,"[184] Hillary called it, as she and Tipper waved at crowds gathered by the roadside and talked with each other about their experiences as political wives. The foursome also flew around the country to raise money, give speeches, and just sit down and talk with folks. These impromptu chats gave them a chance to learn about issues on voters' minds.

They also gave Hillary the opportunity to share the message she'd learned from her childhood minister, Reverend Jones. "To be a Christian did not just mean you were concerned about your own personal salvation,"[185] she said. You were supposed to do good in the world.

While Chelsea's parents were on the road and in the air that fall, the twelve-year-old stayed in Little Rock. But she talked with them every day by telephone, in various hotels or airports. One evening in McAllen, Texas, fifteen aides and supporters waited impatiently on the jet for Hillary to board so they could fly to their next rally. After an hour, a local politician exclaimed, "I'm not waiting anymore." He stomped off the plane and into the terminal. When he overheard the conversation between Hillary and Chelsea, he returned sheepishly. "They're doing homework,"[186] he said.

Throughout the grueling campaign, Bill's poll numbers generally went up, meaning that his chance of winning seemed to improve. President Bush had angered his constituents when he raised income taxes after promising not to. And Perot talked mostly about schools and business but not much else. With two opponents running against Bill, though, the vote could still go any which way.

During the final twenty-four hours of the race, Hillary and Bill hopped in and out of Pennsylvania, Ohio, Michigan, Missouri, Kentucky, Texas, New Mexico, and Colorado before returning to Little Rock. On November 4, 1992, they voted there.

By eleven o'clock that night, the country knew Bill had won. Although less than half—only 43 percent—of the public supported him, he had earned the majority of the electoral college vote. President George H. W. Bush called to concede the election.

. . . .

THE ELECTORAL COLLEGE

When voters go to the polls, they don't actually vote for a presidential candidate. Instead, they vote for electors to represent them in the electoral college. It is this body (which isn't really a college) that selects the president of the United States. This system was established by the men who wrote the Constitution. Every state has as many electors as it has members in Congress; the District of Columbia also gets three. So there are a total of 538 electors.

The presidential candidate who receives the majority of their votes wins, even if that person did not win the majority of the votes in the country. That happened in 1992, when more than half the citizens voted for President George H. W. Bush plus Ross Perot. Bill Clinton received less than half the votes but he won in the majority of the states with large electoral votes.

. . . .

"Bill and I went into our bedroom," Hillary said, "closed the door, and prayed together for God's help as he took on this awesome honor and responsibility."[187]

When they emerged, their friends from Park Ridge, Wellesley, Yale, and elsewhere joined tens of thousands of supporters in town and cheered the president-elect and the First Lady-to-be.

"Hail to the Chief"

The first time Hillary saw the White House, in 1958, she was ten years old, and she peered between the railings of the wrought-iron fence erected to protect the First Family from intruders. Twenty years later, she dined there with President Jimmy Carter. On January 20, 1993, Hillary Rodham Clinton and her husband and daughter moved in.

The incoming president's inaugural events began days before the official ceremony. The Clintons and the Gores rode a bus from Monticello, President Thomas Jefferson's home in Charlottesville, Virginia, to an outdoor festival on the Washington Mall. Bob Dylan, whose song Hillary had studied with her youth group, performed a concert. So did the folk musician Judy Collins, who sang "Chelsea Morning." Bill led a bell-ringing ceremony that cascaded around the country and even in a space shuttle circling the earth. And Hillary made sure there were special activities for kids, featuring puppets, and for teens, rock music.

On the morning of the inauguration—a bracingly cold, clear day—Hillary attended events in her honor at the local Wellesley and Yale Clubs. Afterward, however, she got stuck in traffic. Afraid of showing up late for the ceremony, she leaped out of the limousine and raced back to change clothes. Her startled Secret Service agents chased after her. Fortunately, she made it on time.

Thousands of Arkansans had descended on DC. FOHs and FOBs received reserved seats. Steve, Hillary's colleague from Fayetteville, watched Bill emerge from the US Capitol building as the Marine Band played "Hail to the Chief."

It's just the Clintons! he thought. "We didn't get the gravity of it,"[188] he later admitted.

· ·

NEW NAMES

With Bill's inauguration, the Secret Service designated new official code names for the Clintons. The President was referred to as "Eagle" or POTUS—President of the United States. Hillary became "Evergreen" or FLOTUS—First Lady of the United States. And Chelsea was called "Energy."

· ·

Hillary, however, "felt moved beyond words"[189] to hear that stately piece played for her husband. Wearing a royal-blue coat and matching wide-brimmed hat, she held a family Bible on which Bill placed his hand. He swore to "preserve, protect, and defend the Constitution of the United States."

Bill gave an address about the value of public service. Maya Angelou read poetry, and a choir from Little Rock sang. After a luncheon, the president and First Lady rode in a limousine and walked the parade route along Pennsylvania Avenue.

Meanwhile, during the six-hour event, the chief usher at the White House had the Bushes' possessions moved out and the Clintons' belongings moved in. By the time the First Family arrived at their new home, their clothes were hung in the closets, favorite snacks stashed in the pantry, and photos placed on the walls.

That's when it hit Hillary. "I was actually the First Lady, married to the president of the United States."[190]

Hillary, in a violet lace and chiffon gown, and Bill, in a tuxedo, put in appearances at ten gala balls that evening, dancing until after two in the morning. Her friend Jinnet was honored to be seated at dinner next to

Vice President Al Gore, who talked about a new concept called "the internet."

The first party, though, was Chelsea's. She and her friends learned their way around the 132-room mansion by following clues in a scavenger hunt prepared by the staff. One clue read, "Find the secret staircase."[191] They also discovered a ramp on which they could slide from the solarium down to the family residence.

"You've Got to Protect Chelsea"

Hillary wanted Chelsea to have a normal childhood while growing up at 1600 Pennsylvania Avenue. Shortly after the inauguration, she visited with former First Lady Jacqueline Kennedy Onassis, whose children were young when her husband, John F. Kennedy, was president.

"You've got to protect Chelsea at all costs," Jackie urged. "Keep the press away."[192]

One way to accomplish this goal was to send Chelsea to a private, rather than a public, school. "Private schools were private property," Hillary explained, "hence off-limits to the news media."[193] Chelsea enrolled in

Sidwell Friends, a Quaker school.

To reinforce the message, the president's press aide informed journalists that they were not to cover Chelsea. They grumbled but agreed to leave her alone, except when she appeared in public with her parents.

• •

HILLARY INCOGNITO

As First Lady, Hillary was one of the most recognizable women in America. "I do sometimes wish I could just go for a walk in New York and go unnoticed,"[194] she yearned. And one day, that happened! As she strolled through a museum, a woman stopped her and said, "You sure look like Hillary Clinton." The First Lady responded, "So I'm told."[195]

Would she really rather be unknown? "Whatever minor inconveniences my situation presents," she later said, "I wouldn't trade it for the world."[196]

• •

Hillary could no longer hop in the family hatchback to pick Chelsea up from school. "Everyday experiences that millions of Americans took for granted became extraordinary for me,"[197] she said. Still, she made sure she was home most afternoons when Chelsea returned to the White House and went to Parent-Teacher Association (PTA) meetings and ballet recitals.

To make the residence feel homey, Hillary had a fancy chef's kitchen converted into an eat-in kitchen for family meals. An area off the master bedroom became their family room, with a television set and game table. And Hillary scattered plump sofas around the solarium for Chelsea's slumber parties.

These were the jobs that Hillary the Mom focused on as the family made the transition from Arkansas to Washington. She had other important responsibilities as well, especially serving as First Lady.

"The Biggest Problem"

The position of First Lady does not come with a job description or, as Hillary joked, a "training manual."[198] In fact, she said, "It's not a job; it's a role."[199] She'd held jobs since she was a teenager, and she wasn't used to not working. Actually, as First Lady, she would be expected to work hard—for no pay. But the tasks were assigned to her because of her husband's success, not her own.

Shortly after moving into the White House in January, for instance, Hillary was surprised to learn that she already had to choose a theme, decorations, music, and cards for next Christmas!

Each First Lady has molded the role to fit her particular priorities, ambitions, and skills. Generally, presidents' wives have tended to social functions at the White House while also bringing attention to issues they care about, such as the beauty of the environment (Lady Bird Johnson) and literacy (Laura Bush). Several First Ladies also influenced policy. Rosalind Carter, for instance, attended cabinet meetings and testified before Congress about mental health issues. Edith Wilson became an unofficial copresident after her husband, Woodrow, suffered a stroke.

Hillary's role model was Eleanor Roosevelt, wife of Franklin Delano Roosevelt. She spoke out forcefully about her own political views in press conferences, lectures, radio broadcasts, congressional testimony, and a daily newspaper column. Hillary especially appreciated Mrs. Roosevelt's advice that "every woman in political life needs to develop skin as tough as rhinoceros hide."[200]

ELEANOR ROOSEVELT

From the 1930s through the 1950s, Eleanor Roosevelt was considered one of the most powerful women in America. Although she was born into a prominent and wealthy family, she fought for ordinary people and women's rights. She was the first wife of a president to hold all-female press conferences and to speak at a national political convention.

In 1939, Mrs. Roosevelt shocked segregationists. First, she sat next to black people at a meeting in Alabama. Then, she arranged for Marian Anderson, a black woman, to sing at the Lincoln Memorial. After her husband's death, she was appointed America's representative to the United Nations, where she directed the development of the Universal Declaration of Human Rights.

As a lawyer, political activist, and policy advisor, Hillary had many priorities, ambitions, and skills. What, she wondered, should she do?

Hillary and Bill discussed the country's most pressing

needs. The economy was in a slump. Perhaps she could work on that. She also pondered the issues she had devoted herself to—women and children, education, health care—and recalled hard-luck stories she'd heard on the campaign trail. A woman in New Hampshire told her she couldn't afford the medication her doctor prescribed. Hillary knew many people faced this predicament.

Nearly 37 million Americans had no health insurance in 1993, and approximately the same number didn't have enough insurance. That was about one-fourth of the country's population. Medically related expenses cost Americans $800 billion a year, amounting to nearly one-seventh of the national economy.

A more efficient health-care system could save the public and the government as much as $67 billion every year. It could help fix the economy *and* people's medical problems at the same time.

Hillary and Bill agreed that she should overhaul America's vast and complex health industry. Friends and advisors agreed this was a worthy cause. They encouraged her to give talks, write articles, and hold conferences—three of the typical ways that previous women in her position had called attention to their concerns.

Hillary was not satisfied with these methods, however. Yes, speeches and meetings could focus public attention on the issues. But she wanted to change laws, not just attitudes.

Bill recalled what Hillary had achieved as head of the Education Standards Committee when he was governor of Arkansas. "I took the biggest problem I had and put the best person in charge of it," he said, according to an aide. "And it was the most important accomplishment of my term."[201]

Rather than limit her actions to those of traditional First Ladies, Bill appointed Hillary head of the President's Task Force on National Health Care Reform. The goal of the task force was universal health care—lifelong medical care and adequate insurance for every American.

No previous First Lady had ever taken responsibility for creating policy in such a powerful and sweeping way. This effort would be the most ambitious undertaking of Hillary's career. She and Bill would not be copresidents but, by voting him into office, the public would get her leadership skills for free. The physical and financial health of tens of millions of Americans would depend on her succeeding.

"I understood," Hillary said, "that this could be a disaster, that I could get blamed . . . That didn't bother me. Heat comes with anything. If I had done nothing, I would have gotten heat. So better to get heat trying to do something important for people."[202]

Hillary was continuing to take action. Given her touchy relationship with the media, however, this was a risky move.

CHAPTER 6

Calamities in the White House
1993–1994

. . . .

East Wing/West Wing

When most people think of the White House, the image they probably have in mind is the grand central portion, the north side of which faces Pennsylvania Avenue. This is the residence, where the First Family lives on the second and third floors and where formal meetings of state are held on the first floor.

The White House is more than a home. It is also where the president and his (or her) staff work. Hillary once said that, like a small shopkeeper, the president lives over the store.

Actually, the president conducts work in the Oval

Office and other spaces that are in an annex to the residence, called the West Wing. Top advisors debate and develop policies, legislation, and political strategies here. The West Wing is the heart of the executive branch of American government.

The East Wing, on the other side of the residence, contains the offices of the social staff of the White House, such as the calligraphers who pen invitations. The First Lady also has work space in the East Wing. Usually.

As head of the Task Force on National Health Care Reform, Hillary decided that she deserved and needed an office in the West Wing, alongside the president's other policy makers. Her work area was not fancy, merely a small corner on the second floor with a window that overlooked the roof. Nevertheless, this was another of her firsts. Both symbolically and actually, Hillary leaped from the etiquette side of the White House to the power side.

"It was path-breaking,"[203] an official said.

Her staff, an unusually large group of over thirty people—all but one of them women—had offices in a large structure called the Old Executive Office

Building (OEOB) next to the West Wing. They worked alongside and often with the president's policy advisors. Their area, Suite 100, became known as Hillaryland.

Mismanaged Care

Hillary and an aide, Ira Magaziner, started to work on health care within days after the inauguration. They had to. The president had announced that the task force would make its recommendations to Congress, complete with proposed legislation, within one hundred days—by May 1, 1993. Why one hundred? Because sixty years earlier, Franklin Delano Roosevelt had pushed fifteen major bills through Congress in that time. He introduced a New Deal to America. Hillary's work would need to be equally monumental and swift.

It was doable, she believed, because she, Bill, and Ira had already outlined the new system, called "managed care." Working people would continue to get health insurance through their employers, who would join alliances to keep costs down. The federal government would set standards for care and make sure that people without jobs were covered. The six hundred members of the task force, who were experts in the complexities of health care, were divided into committees and charged with figuring out the details.

• •

QUESTIONS ABOUT HEALTH CARE

Before Congress passed President Obama's Affordable Care Act in 2010, Americans spent more money on their medical care than any other country. Yet, of the world's major democracies, the United States had the largest percentage of people with no insurance. Trying to fix these problems in 1993, President Clinton's Task Force on National Health Care Reform debated hundreds of thorny issues. These included:

- Should medical coverage be a government program? Or should Americans continue to get insurance through their employers? Or a combination?
- How should unemployed or retired people get insurance?
- How should doctors be paid—according to the number of patients they see or according to the number of procedures they order?
- If everyone has insurance and can go to the doctor, will there be enough doctors? Will care have to be rationed? If so, by whom?

- How should hospitals decide how much to charge? What about companies that make drugs?
- Who sets standards to be sure medical care is safe and effective?

· ·

Crammed into semifurnished, dimly lit cubicles in the OEOB, committees met six or seven days a week, sometimes for up to eighteen hours. To prevent drafts of the plan from leaking out before it was ready, the gatherings were secret. Hillary knew how to keep a lid on deliberations from her days working with the committee that investigated President Nixon. She was so successful that even the person whose office was directly across the hall from hers in the West Wing had no idea what was happening behind her closed doors. No one outside the process even knew who was on the task force.

Hillary reveled in her job overseeing their discussions. She knew she was doing something important when about eight hundred thousand people from around the country wrote her letters describing their problems with getting medical care. They wrote about being impoverished by catastrophic illnesses or mental health issues; about losing insurance when they lost or switched jobs; about the anguish and expense of caring for aging parents.

One uninsured mother said, "It breaks my heart that I can't allow my children to play sports because if they had an accident, we couldn't cover the costs."[204] As a former tomboy, Hillary thought that was a shame.

The Hillaryland staff posted a giant photograph of her holding seven-year-old Ryan Moore, who was born with dwarfism. She said that looking at his picture "kept our eyes on the prize . . . to bring health-care coverage to all Americans."[205]

At first, the public admired her efforts. Popular magazines portrayed her as the woman who had it all—marriage, family, and a career—the goal she had discussed with her friends at Wellesley. *Time* said, "Hillary Rodham Clinton is the most powerful First Lady in history"[206] and named her "an icon of American womanhood."[207]

The praise didn't last long, however. In February, a group of doctors sued. Like insurance companies and the pharmaceuticals laboratories that develop new drugs, they had been excluded from the task force and wanted a seat at the table. Legislation called "sunshine laws," they pointed out, required that government meetings at which policy is developed must be open to the public. Furthermore, who gave the First Lady the right to head a secret task force? She was merely a private citizen.

Hillary considered the lawsuit more of a nuisance than a threat, even after a federal judge ruled against her. "If you lived your life trying to make sure that nobody ever criticized you," she retorted, "you would probably never get out of bed—and then you'd be criticized for that."[208]

The lawsuit, though, raised two important questions: Can the government develop massive programs affecting tens of millions of Americans, in secret? And what, exactly, is a First Lady allowed to do—and not do? The judge's decision meant that Hillary could no longer attend the meetings of her own task force.

From then on, the process to reform health care resembled the Great Wall of China. Public opinion went uphill and down. The secrecy kept out curiosity-seekers, including members of Congress, who would be asked to vote on it. And it antagonized adversaries.

Some of those opponents were scheming to tear down not only health care but also Hillary and Bill. Calling themselves the No Name Coalition, they were working in secret too—so secretly that Hillary didn't know about their plot.

The health-care plan didn't take as long to construct as the Great Wall did, but by the end of April 1993, it was clear that one hundred days were not nearly enough. The task force was disbanded. Health reform was sidelined while the president focused on other priorities, in particular the economy. Meanwhile, Hillary endured two personal tragedies.

More Heartbreaks

In mid-March, Hillary's father, Hugh, suffered a stroke. She and Chelsea rushed to the hospital in Little Rock. Although Hillary left her work behind, she carried her concerns with her. Facing the possibility of paying for round-the-clock nursing for him, she said, "made me realize what a totally devastating experience health-care problems are for people and how everybody suffers in silence."[209]

Hugh died in early April. His funeral took place on Good Friday, and he was buried in Scranton, his hometown. His death led Hillary to question the purpose of her own life. Only several months earlier, she had told a journalist, "As a Christian, part of my obligation is to take action to alleviate suffering."[210] Still grieving, she returned to Washington determined to alleviate suffering by establishing universal health care.

Two and a half months later, Hillary's good friend from her days at the Rose Law Firm, Vince Foster, shot himself. Hillary reeled, wondering if she was responsible for his suicide. She had urged him to accept the job of deputy White House counsel, lawyer to the president. But Vince found that neither the work nor Washington, DC, suited him. He suffered from depression, and, as an upstanding lawyer, he felt trapped and mortified when the press accused him of mishandling the Clintons' legal matters.

Shortly after moving to Washington, Hillary heard rumors about the White House staff that made airline reservations for reporters who traveled with the president. It sounded as if the financial records were a mess. Busy with the task force, she ordered Vince to "fix it."[211] When the staff was fired, possibly without cause, the *Wall Street Journal* published editorials accusing the president's administration of "carelessness about following the law."[212]

In a note, Vince wrote, "Here ruining people is considered sport."[213] Anguished that she had brought him to a city where he didn't belong and then ignored his despair, Hillary called her first six months in the White House "brutal."[214]

"I Didn't Come to Washington to . . . Compromise"

Despite these setbacks, Hillary seemed to reach the summit of the health-care mountain in September 1993. Summarizing the goals of her plan in a speech before both houses of Congress, the president praised her as having a "rigorous mind, a steady compass, a caring heart."[215] Everyone in the chamber rose, turned toward Hillary, who was seated in the visitors' gallery, and applauded. She nodded and smiled.

The following week, she went to Capitol Hill and testified before five House and Senate committees. Other

First Ladies had spoken to Congressional committees; however, before Hillary, none had presented a comprehensive program she had developed herself.

"I'm here as a mother, a wife, a daughter, a sister, a woman," she stated. "I'm here as an American citizen concerned about the health of her family and the health of her nation."[216]

Over three days, members of Congress grilled her about costs, mandates, and government bureaucracy. Without consulting notes or her staff, she responded fully to every question. A Senate aide found her fearless, just as a colleague had when she campaigned in South Texas. The *New York Times* reported that she "dazzled" the committees. The *Washington Post* called her a "superstar."[217] A Republican senator promised, "We will pass a law next year."[218]

Her presentation on health care seemed as persuasive as her testimony about education before the Arkansas legislature had been. And that had resulted in sweeping reform laws. She was hopeful that health-care reform would also succeed.

At a lawmaker's request, Hillary shared a copy of the unfinished plan. That step backfired, however, when the draft spread to others in Congress. A Democratic senator from New York, Daniel Patrick Moynihan, called her cost estimates "fantasy"[219] numbers. Another complained that she didn't understand how the Senate works—by discussion and cooperation. Hillary was taken aback. Democrats were supposed to be her allies!

Worse, "Harry and Louise" showed up. An actor and actress playing a married couple in television advertisements complained about managed care. An announcer intoned, "The government may force us to pick from a few health-care plans designed by government bureaucrats." Harry said, "They choose." Louise added, "We lose."[220]

Paid for by insurance companies that opposed the plan, the ads suggested that federal government workers, rather than doctors, would make medical decisions if Hillary's recommendations were adopted. The ads were misleading but many people, even those who needed health insurance, believed them.

Some of Hillary's colleagues warned her that her plan might not pass Congress after all. Carol Rasco, a friend from Little Rock who had become Bill's domestic policy advisor, proposed an alternative.

"Instead of trying to do the big picture," she said, "let's go for children."[221] In case Congress failed to pass the entire program, Carol urged development of a package that would at least cover poor kids. Donna Shalala, the secretary of health and human services, concurred and offered to help. They tried to persuade Hillary to shrink her goal. Determined to cover everyone, however, Hillary refused.

Republicans, too, proposed a compromise—a bill that would cover *most* people, about 85 percent. By joining with Democrats, they even rounded up enough votes that it might pass. Bill agreed that that was a good idea and prepared to negotiate. White House aides heard Hillary shouting at him.

"I didn't come to Washington to . . . compromise," she asserted. "You're either for universal coverage or you're not."[222] The president backed away from the negotiating table.

Knowing that she was feeling stressed, Hillaryland sprung a surprise forty-sixth birthday party for her on October 26. Staffers disguised as "a dozen different Hillarys"[223]—baking cookies, fixing health care, flipping her hair—had her don a Dolley Madison outfit of black wig and hoop skirt. Bill appeared as President James Madison, wearing a white wig and tights. She loved the getups and the frivolity but decided that Bill "looks better in a suit."[224]

"My Brain Aches"

On October 27, 1993—180 days late—the White House submitted Hillary's Health Security Act to Congress. It ran 1,342 pages. Hardly anyone besides Hillary and Ira knew what it contained, and even they weren't sure what it would cost. Studying the details, Bill confessed, "My brain aches."[225]

Everyone could find something in the act to hate. Republicans claimed that families that already had good insurance would lose it. Doctors charged that the plan would ruin medical practice. Democrats complained that it would cost too much. Harry and Louise popped up again. In two months, public enthusiasm for health reform plummeted from two-thirds of the country to less than one half.

At that point, the legislation got stalled. And Hillary

and Bill got distracted when reporters raised questions about Hillary's long-ago financial dealings.

"Poring Over Our Personal Lives"

Back in Arkansas, Hillary and Bill had lost money in the vacation-home business, Whitewater Development Corporation. But investigators suspected that they might have benefitted from illegal actions by their partner, Jim McDougal. If so, they might have been involved in a conflict of interest. Reporters and government examiners pressed Hillary to hand over her financial records. Knowing she was innocent, she refused.

"I don't want them poring over our personal lives,"[226] she explained, believing that the president had the right to a private life. In any case, she couldn't find all of the paperwork. It had somehow been misplaced when she and Bill moved from the governor's mansion to the White House.

Republicans smelled something fishy. Some even suggested that Vince Foster knew she was guilty— so she arranged to have him murdered and make his death look like a suicide! They demanded that the president have Attorney General Janet Reno name a special prosecutor—a lawyer who investigates government officials suspected of committing a crime.

Hillary knew from her experience working on the Nixon case that a special prosecutor has the right to look into everything, forever. They would never have any privacy. She begged Bill: do not appoint a special prosecutor!

Convinced that Hillary was covering something up, news outlets went after her. Again, they portrayed her as polarizing—someone who seemed to be a do-gooder but was really a troublemaker. The *New York Times* said she saw herself as a "saint"[227] but that she came across as a finger-wagging preacher. Her old friends didn't recognize the person depicted by the press. A college classmate, Nancy Gist, said, "It was shocking to me to see the difference between the person who I knew and the person who was caricatured in the media."[228]

Hillary felt under siege. Now *she* was the one who smelled something fishy. She claimed that right-wing Republicans were behind the media frenzy. However, no one else saw any evidence for that. A member of

Bill's cabinet said of the Clintons, "They've become paranoid. They think people are out to get them."[229]

Over her protests, Bill had Reno appoint a special prosecutor. He figured that they'd be found innocent, and the case would be closed. Bill was partially right. By the summer of 1994, this official, Robert Fiske Jr., cleared everyone of wrongdoing.

But the case wasn't closed. In August, another lawyer, Kenneth W. Starr, was appointed special prosecutor in Fiske's place. Starr ordered Hillary to hand over the records she couldn't find.

"I Felt in Real Physical Danger"

Trying to rally support for the health-care act that summer, Hillary launched a cross-country bus caravan called the "Health Security Express." Buses would transport sick people and their doctors, known as "Reform Riders," to Washington, DC, where they'd lobby Congress to vote for the bill. Hillary wept when one rider explained that his wife had just died of cancer because they had no insurance.

"Unless we can assure universal health coverage to all

Americans, then life, liberty, and the pursuit of happiness for some is just a dream,"[230] he said.

Along the route, however, opponents repeatedly got the upper hand. In Portland, Oregon, challengers blockaded the bus. Low-flying planes trailed banners emblazoned "Phony Express." In Seattle, Washington, over two thousand militants, some carrying holstered guns and knives, drowned out Hillary's speech by screaming catcalls. Hundreds swarmed her car. She was relieved her Secret Service agents had persuaded her to wear a bulletproof vest.

"I felt in real physical danger,"[231] she admitted. "They had such hatred on their faces."[232]

"We Conceded Defeat"

Guns? Bulletproof vest? Hatred? All Hillary wanted to do was make sure everyone could see a doctor when they got sick. What was the matter with that?

The matter was an issue Hillary had been struggling with since high school—how big should government be?

The Harry and Louise ads exaggerated how much power the federal government would have if her act passed. Nevertheless, the bureaucracy would grow under her omnibus plan. Furthermore, her my-way-or-the-highway attitude showed that the executive branch would not bargain on this point.

To shrink government, conservative leaders resolved to kill the Health Security Act. If it passed, a strategist named William Kristol predicted, people would become dependent on the government's dime. Not only that, but they'd like having health insurance so much they'd keep voting for Democrats, and Republicans would never take back the White House or Congress! Kristol argued that preventing the bill from passing—and blaming Hillary for its failure—would reduce the size of government, get rid of the Clintons, and return the Republicans to power. That would be three wins for the conservative team!

It turned out that Hillary's suspicions about right-wing activists were accurate. Members of the No Name Coalition had secretly conspired to run the Health Security Express off the road and the Health Security Act into the ground. They planted protesters along the buses' routes; handed out bumper stickers reading "Government Health Care Makes Me Sick"; sent scripts opposing the act to radio talk show hosts; and arranged for two thousand callers to bombard members of Congress.

Their tactics were successful, and the bill lost support. In August 1994, Hillary was finally ready to compromise. But it was too late. Kristol and others persuaded every Republican in Congress, even the ones whose constituents wanted insurance, to stop negotiating and to vote against health-care reform.

In September 1994, "health care faded with barely a whimper," Hillary said. "After twenty months, we conceded defeat."[233] She was devastated. Republicans rejoiced.

What Went Wrong?

Throughout those twenty months, Hillary believed she was acting with the best of intentions.

"We came here to do good things," she said, "and we just didn't understand so many things about this town."[234] She was not used to making mistakes. In the end, she admitted, "I knew I had contributed to our failure."[235]

A busload of reasons has been cited for that failure; they continue to be debated. Many of them are related to actions or inaction by the president and members of Congress. Here are several related to Hillary. She thought deeply about where she went wrong and what she could learn from her blunders.

Creating a Task Force

Other strategies were possible. For instance, Congress could have developed the plan. However, Hillary was determined to establish managed care and universal coverage, and Congress might have had other ideas. Politicians, she learned, have to develop the best strategies to reach their goals. Along the way, they might have to adjust both the strategies *and* the goals.

Putting the First Lady in Charge

Because Hillary was the wife of the president of the United States, staffers hesitated to disagree with her. And when Bill disagreed with her, he couldn't fire her.

However, Hillary was qualified to lead the effort, and she wanted to expand the role of the First Lady, as Eleanor Roosevelt had done. After all, she had accomplished such work as the First Lady of Arkansas.

But "the difference between being a governor's wife and a president's is immeasurable,"[236] she discovered. "I underestimated the resistance I would meet as a First Lady with a policy mission,"[237] she later said. Apparently, the country was not ready for an outspoken, policy-setting, feminist First Spouse. People who are not elected to office but who have power anyway, she learned, need to decide the best way to use that power.

Hillary's Refusal to Compromise

If Hillary had negotiated with Republicans early on, a law that gave most Americans health insurance might have passed and would have been better than no law.

"Our most critical mistake," Hillary later conceded, "was trying to do too much too fast."[238] Since Bill had been elected with only 43 percent of the vote, he didn't have the public's support for sweeping changes.

However, Hillary had made a pledge to the American people for universal health care. And she didn't want to break her promise. Politicians, Hillary learned, have to decide when to remain true to their principles and when to make trade-offs.

Working in Secret

Secrecy created suspicion, frustration, and confusion. However, Hillary knew that the task force needed to hash out ideas in private before the public had a chance to bash them. Politicians, Hillary learned, have to decide when to work behind closed doors and when to listen to other people's opinions.

Was the Health Security Act Doomed?

Perhaps right-wingers would have defeated health care no matter what Hillary or anyone else did. They set a trap, and the Democrats drove right in.

After eighteen years in Arkansas, she knew how the state operated. Yet she had plunged into a massive legislative program after only a week in Washington. A historian wrote that Washington is not "a three-ring circus but a thousand-ring circus."[239] Furthermore, as her friend Steve said, "Washington has sharper teeth."[240]

Hillary tried to "do all the good" she could, as John Wesley directed, by striving to overhaul America's health-care system. However, she didn't use "all the means" she could. She admitted, "I'm confused. I just don't know what works anymore."[241]

To continue doing good, she'd have to figure out what works and change her methods.

"It Was a Slaughter"

"Sweeping Gains for Republicans."[242]

"Voters Are Fed Up."[243]

"Democrats Go Down."[244]

These were a few of the newspaper headlines on November 10, 1994. Two days earlier, Americans had gone to the polls to vote for their representatives and senators. Democrats lost fifty-four members in the House of Representatives and eight senators. Republicans became the majority party in Congress for the first time in forty years.

"It was a slaughter," one White House official said. "People were wandering around in a daze."[245]

· ·

ADMINISTRATION ACCOMPLISHMENTS

Although pollsters had predicted that Republicans would take over Congress in 1994, President Clinton was still surprised and frustrated by the extent of Democrats' losses.

He had thought that voters would appreciate his administration's achievements in its first two years. These included:

- The Family and Medical Leave Act, which allowed workers to take leave from their jobs for family emergencies and the birth or adoption of a child
- A peace agreement between longtime enemies, Israel and the Palestine Liberation Organization
- The Violent Crime Control and Law Enforcement Act, which protected women and others against violent crimes
- The North America Free Trade Agreement among countries in the Western Hemisphere
- The National Voter Registration Act, which expanded voter registration
- The Deficit Reduction Act, which reduced the national debt and created millions of new jobs
- The Brady Handgun Violence Prevention Act, which required a background check for people who wanted to buy a handgun
- Creation of AmeriCorps for young people to earn college tuition by working in their communities

• •

There were many reasons for the electoral losses. The public was upset that the president hadn't improved the economy. And they didn't like rumors they heard about his behavior with other women.

Hillary, too, blamed herself for her missteps with health care. "I faulted myself,"[246] she confessed. Morose but also angry, she sought help in several places.

She went to Sunday services regularly at Foundry United Methodist Church, near the White House. Bible readings and her prayer group, composed mainly of the wives of both Democratic and Republican congressmen, helped sustain her.

Friends gave her a book that contained a striking phrase: "the discipline of gratitude." It hit her over the head, she said, "like a shovel . . . I had never thought of gratitude as a habit or discipline before."[247]

She began to make a mental list of things she was grateful for. Chelsea, of course, topped the list. Another item was "the awesome privilege of working on behalf of my country."[248] She wanted to continue to do this work, though she wasn't sure how.

She turned to her friends and colleagues in Hillary-land for guidance.

CHAPTER 7

The White House: Hillary Abroad
1995

• •

"Soldier On"

Several weeks after the catastrophic midterm elections in November 1994, Hillary sat down with ten of her staff members—a subgroup of Hillarylanders dubbed "the Chix."[249] They gathered in the White House Map Room, where President Franklin Delano Roosevelt had planned the Allies' assault on Germany during World War II. Hillary was not plotting military maneuvers—but she definitely needed a new strategy as First Lady.

She stifled tears as she apologized for her mistakes over the past two years. She felt she "had let everyone down and contributed to our losses."[250] She promised that it wouldn't happen again. In fact, she was considering giving up political work entirely.

The Chix listened respectfully. Then Hillary's speechwriter, Lissa Muscatine, responded, "Young people look to you for guidance in their own lives . . . What kind of message would you be sending if you stopped being actively involved?"[251]

Although Hillary was tempted to retreat, she realized Lissa was right and resolved to "soldier on."[252] The question was: What should she do now? Heading a task force and writing legislation had certainly backfired.

She conferred with several people—including her idol, who had died in 1962! "I had imaginary conversations with Mrs. Roosevelt," Hillary admitted. Looking at her photograph, Hillary recalled her heroine's wise words: "A woman is like a tea bag. You never know how strong she is until she's in hot water."[253] Reporters made fun of Hillary, claiming that she was trying to commune with dead people. Since she still hadn't developed rhino hide, she got irritated at them.

Dick Morris, a political consultant, took a poll and advised her that Americans wanted a traditional First Lady—an advocate rather than a policy maker.[254] As a longtime supporter of children, women, and families, Hillary knew that role fit her well. She could focus attention on their needs by giving talks, writing articles, and holding conferences—yes, the same three traditional methods her friends had suggested when she moved into the White House.

Sounding like Tammy Wynette, the singer who stood by her man, Hillary described her new role. "My first responsibility," she said, "is to do whatever my husband would want me to do."[255]

She stopped participating in policy sessions and rarely appeared in the West Wing. Nevertheless, although she followed the usual paths taken by former First Ladies, Hillary literally took them in new directions.

. . . .

HOW DID THE FIRST LADY FLY?

When the First Lady flew without the president, she was assigned a military plane comfortably fitted out with seats that recline into flat beds, and often with showers. She sometimes used a recycled Air Force One. But if the vice president needed it for a diplomatic mission, she was bumped to a different plane.

Fortunately, her pilots were among the best trained in the world. One wintry night, they landed in Siberia on an unpaved, unlighted runway. At takeoff, men de-iced the wings with shovels.

• •

"Borders Don't Need to Be Boundaries"

Hillary recalled that, to help families in Arkansas, she and Bill had imported programs from other countries.

"She felt that we had a lot to give to other places and a lot to gain from other places," Lissa said. "Borders don't need to be boundaries."[256] Ideas flow every which way. Looking at the drawings in the Map Room, Hillary had a revelation. Many of the countries where women were discriminated against were the poorest and most troubled on earth. Those were the places she needed to visit.

In March 1995, Hillary and fifteen-year-old Chelsea traveled through five countries in South Asia. The Secret Service fervently wished that Evergreen and Energy would call only on leaders in well-guarded palaces. But Hillary was intent on visiting with women in city slums and rural villages as well.

Their first stop was the capital of Pakistan—Islamabad, a planned city built thirty years earlier atop the remains of ancient civilizations. Immediately Hillary and Chelsea confronted extreme contrasts of ancient and modern, wealthy and impoverished.

The president's wife, called the Begum, lived in *purdah*, which meant that she rarely ventured beyond her residence and was never allowed to see—or be seen by—a man outside her family. Yet Pakistan had a female prime minister, Benazir Bhutto, who had studied at Harvard and Oxford Universities. Talking with this sophisticated leader, Hillary said she felt "rocketed forward several centuries."[257]

Hillary asked her to convene a group of women from different backgrounds to discuss their dreams for their country. She not only learned about their lives, but also hoped they would continue their conversations after she left.

The Americans brought medicines to a remote village with no electricity. Entire families lived in single rooms. Visiting a primary school for girls, they were saddened to learn that the students would not be allowed to attend secondary school.

By contrast, mother and daughter, dressed one night in vivid silk *shalwar kameez*, dined at a banquet in a fortress lit by thousands of oil lamps. They were entertained by fireworks displays, strolling musicians, and camels draped in jeweled robes.

"Silence"

In New Delhi, India, Hillary and Chelsea held babies wearing colorful outfits in an orphanage run by Mother Teresa. This tiny, saintly woman took in infants, many of whom were girls abandoned by their parents, simply because they were girls. It was this attitude— that females are worthless—that Hillary yearned to change.

The next day, a school principal handed her a poem titled "Silence." It was composed by Anasuya Sengupta, a senior at the school, and calligraphed as beautifully as an invitation to the White House. Hillary was so struck by its message that she asked Lissa to help her make "Silence" the centerpiece of a speech she was to give that evening.

"Discussion of such problems as education and health care for girls and women is viewed by some as 'soft,'"[258] Hillary told her audience. Leaders don't consider these issues as serious as, say, war. However, she explained, "where women prosper, countries prosper."[259]

She concluded her talk by quoting Anasuya's poem: "Too many women in too many countries speak the same language—of silence . . . And yet, there must be freedom—if we are to speak. And yes, there must be power—if we are to be heard."[260] The value of women's voices became Hillary's refrain that night and from then on.

The audience was touched by her message. So was the American press corps that traveled with her. The *New York Times* reported that the First Lady, who had become quieter since the failure of her health reform effort, had "found a new voice" herself. The paper also praised Chelsea for showing "exquisite poise."[261] Hillary was pleased that her daughter was developing "a style of her own."[262]

Reporters were allowed to quote Chelsea at the Taj Mahal. Gazing at the magnificent seventeenth-century marble tomb, she said, "When I was little, this was sort of the embodiment of the fairy-tale palace for me. I would see pictures of it and would dream I was a princess or whatever. Now that I'm here it's spectacular."[263]

Although that was the last time they could report on Chelsea, Hillary and the press corps were no longer at war, at least while they traveled together abroad. They appreciated her fervor when she spoke out on women's issues. Chatting with each other on long flights, they heard her famous laugh. Overseas, she was buffered from the right wing's accusations.

To emphasize her point that the well-being of a country depends on the well-being of its women, Hillary and her entourage traveled to the city of Ahmedabad in the Indian state of Gujarat. She wanted to visit the Self-Employed Women's Association (SEWA), an organization that provided training and tiny loans to poverty-stricken women. With the loans—some as little as a dollar—they bought material or seeds and earned money by making kites or raising vegetables to sell.

News of Hillary's planned visit had spread. Nearly a thousand women, some of whom had walked ten or twelve hours on dusty paths, arrived at the organization's one-room office.

"Tears filled my eyes," she said, "when I saw them waiting for me under a large tent." Arrayed in jewel-toned saris, "they looked like an undulating human rainbow."[264]

Many told her that they were proud of the independence they had gained from working at a job and making money. Hillary understood how they felt. As the meeting ended, they rose and sang the American civil rights song "We Shall Overcome" in their native language. Hillary said, "I was overwhelmed and uplifted."[265]

"Human Rights Are Women's Rights"

About every five years, the United Nations held a World Conference on Women. The Fourth Conference was scheduled to take place in Beijing, the capital city of China, in September 1995, and Hillary was asked to lead the American delegation. She was eager to go but feared she would be forced to cancel.

The Chinese leadership, which has a long history

of suppressing free speech, imprisoned a man named Harry Wu for criticizing the government. As a result, members of Congress—including women—and the press pressured Hillary to boycott China. Going there, they argued, would make it appear that America didn't care about the rights of citizens in other countries.

Hillary argued that she cared deeply, especially about the rights of women in every country. She even threatened to rent a rowboat and row across the Pacific Ocean, if necessary!

Fortunately, China released Wu. And Hillary and her companions and staff flew off. During the flight, she reviewed her speech. After reading a draft, Hillary handed it back to Lissa, saying, "I want to push the envelope as far as I can when it comes to women's rights and human rights."[266] The next night, Hillary accomplished that goal.

In the gigantic Great Hall of the People, she stood in front of more than four thousand delegates from 189 countries. She declared,

It is time to break our silence . . . [I]t is no longer acceptable to discuss women's rights as separate from

human rights . . . It is a violation of human rights when babies are denied food . . . simply because they are born girls . . . If there is one message that echoes forth from this conference, it is that human rights are women's rights . . . . And women's rights are human rights . . . God's blessings on you, your work, and all who will benefit from it.[267]

. . . .

HUMAN RIGHTS

"Human rights" refers to the basic rights that are due to every person. The US Constitution lists these as "life, liberty, and the pursuit of happiness." The United Nations refers to several factors, including "dignity and justice for all of us" and "life, liberty, and security of person."[268]

. . . .

Although the delegates had been silent as they listened to their translations, they rose and cheered for more than twenty minutes after she concluded. For many, the idea that, as human beings, women have the same rights as men was revolutionary.

Dozens of newspapers praised her presentation. In an

editorial, the *New York Times* wrote that this "may have been her finest moment in public life."[269]

It wasn't only the media that expressed admiration for Hillary. She acquired an international following on this trip as well. A delegate from Tanzania responded, "She talked so eloquently about human rights . . . All of the women here will know that the wife of the president of the United States also thinks about these things."[270]

The next day, Hillary was driven through a chilling rainstorm to the town of Huairou, an hour northeast of Beijing. A separate conference was held there for thirty thousand representatives from nongovernmental organizations around the world that support women, such as SEWA. It was said to be the largest event for women ever held. Chinese officials had barred them from the conference in Beijing and prevented most attendees from hearing Hillary in Huairou, too.

· ·

NONGOVERNMENTAL ORGANIZATIONS

A nongovernmental organization—or NGO— is one that is neither part of a government agency nor a profit-making business. NGOs are usually created by ordinary citizens for a particular cause, such as supporting women or preventing a disease. They range in size and might have a large budget with paid staff or no money at all and rely on volunteers.

. . . .

Thousands of people stood outside in the mud. One of them was Betty Friedan, who had written *The Feminine Mystique*, the book that sparked the women's movement while Hillary was at Wellesley. The delegates were frustrated at being excluded but they were exhilarated to be together.

"You didn't speak the same language but you would look into another's eyes, and you would hug," Hillary's friend Jan Piercy said. "We were all working for a larger voice for women and the right for women to contribute to the building of their communities and their countries. The energy was remarkable!"[271]

Over a thousand participants crammed into the auditorium. Waiting for Hillary, they sang American civil rights songs. During her talk, she again read Anasuya's poem "Silence." Alyse Nelson, an American college student who heard Hillary, was so inspired that she said, "She has voice and power, and she uses [them] to empower others. I, too, have a voice. I need to use that voice to support others."[272]

Action!

As moving as her presentations in China were, Hillary knew that real change requires more than talk. The delegates at the conference adopted a Platform for Action. Its major goal was full participation by women in society, politics, and the economy. That is, women should have an equal voice with men in making decisions about their lives and their countries. Every nation that was represented agreed to strive for that goal.

After Hillary returned to Washington, she urged government agencies to carry out the plan. For instance, she worked with Madeleine Albright, the first female secretary of state (and another Wellesley alumna), to establish the Vital Voices Democracy Initiative, which trained female leaders. In addition, Hillary helped increase American support for microfinance projects, fighting AIDS (acquired immunodeficiency syndrome), and other issues that affect women.

The trips Hillary made to South Asia and China

were just the beginning. Over the next five years, she traveled throughout Africa, North and South America, Europe, the United Kingdom, the Far East, the South Pacific, and the Middle East. At almost every stop, she held gatherings, which she called "convenings," with women, like the first one in Pakistan. The Americans got insight into the status of women around the world. And local participants began conversations about common goals that continued long after she left.

Hillary also continued to have adventures. Hillary-land staff teased that the State Department decided, "If a place was too small, too dangerous, or too poor—send Hillary."[273]

One time, the prime minister of Slovakia, a former boxer, personally threatened her by moving closer and closer to her on the couch, shaking his fist in her face, and shouting with rage. On another excursion, Hillary and Madeleine held a high-level huddle about confidential diplomatic news in the only private location they could find—a ladies' bathroom.

One afternoon, when Hillary had rare free time, she and her staff disguised themselves as tourists in casual clothes, big hats, and sunglasses and went window-shopping in

Budapest, Hungary. The trick worked until some real American tourists yelled, "Hillary! Hi!"[274]

Possibly the most challenging travel event confronted her at a dinner in Russia when President Boris Yeltsin exclaimed, "Hillary, I have a very special treat for you tonight."

What was the treat? Moose lips soup.

"Sure enough," she said, "floating in the murky broth was my own set of moose lips. The gelatinous shapes looked like rubber bands that had lost their stretch . . . I tasted a lot of unusual food for my country, but I drew the line at moose lips."[275]

In 1997, Hillary returned to India for the funeral of Mother Teresa. A government leader told her, "Mrs. Clinton, we heard you when you were in India [in 1995]. We are investing more in girls' education."[276] She was thrilled that her voice was making an impact. After all, "no democracy, economy or peace agreement can ever fully succeed when one half of a nation's population remains unrepresented."[277]

Three years later, just before she left the White House, Vital Voices moved out of the State Department and became an independent organization. Renamed the

Vital Voices Global Partnership, it holds conferences and trains thousands of women around the world in leadership and economic development. Its president is Alyse Nelson, the college student Hillary had inspired and then mentored.

Successes such as these showed Hillary that she could improve women's lives even without an office in the West Wing.

CHAPTER 8

The White House: Hillary at Home
1993–2000

. . . .

It Takes a Village

From her office in the East Wing and with help from Hillaryland, the First Lady influenced domestic policy. She also had fun living in the White House.

Hillary held convenings not only around the world but at home, too. One afternoon, at a gathering of mothers who worked at a factory in Baltimore, Maryland, a woman looked up at the clock. "Mrs. Clinton," she said, "at three o'clock, I'm filled with worry because that's when my child gets out of school, walks home, gets in the house by himself, and is there alone until I get home. I'm not even allowed to call him to see if he got home safely."[278]

Chelsea had always had safe places to play at the Arkansas governor's mansion and the White House. But Hillary understood that other working parents needed reliable after-school care for their children.

She had already shown her own support for working mothers. She hired her speechwriter, Lissa Muscatine, when Lissa was pregnant with twins—and then let her work from home when she needed to. Hillary also urged Bill to ban discrimination by the federal government against employees who have children. That meant, for example, that a mother could not be turned down for a job in favor of a man who didn't have kids.

Hillary called concerns like these "kitchen-table issues" because they affect people where they matter most—at home. To shine a light on these problems and search for solutions, Hillary used her "bully pulpit." This is a term coined by President Theodore Roosevelt, Eleanor's uncle, to refer to the publicity given to events at the White House. (In the early twentieth century, "bully" meant "wonderful," not "tormenting.") Hillary held conferences on family-friendly topics, like teenagers, childcare, and the development of babies' brains.

ISSUES AROUND THE KITCHEN TABLE

Hillary found lots of ways to support families. She helped persuade Congress to pass the State Children's Health Insurance Program (CHIP) for youngsters whose parents didn't have heath-care coverage. She encouraged parents to immunize children against contagious diseases, like measles. She helped increase funding for the preschool program Head Start and for research on asthma in youth. And she championed Reach Out and Read, a program in which doctors "prescribe" books to babies.

Sometimes Hillary stopped legislation too. She had a staffer track the effects that bills being considered in Congress would have on families. The staff member reported that a bankruptcy bill could make it hard for divorced fathers who were going bankrupt to support their children. Hillary asked Bill to veto it. He did.

Wanting to bring nationwide attention to issues that concern families, Hillary gave an address at the Democratic National Convention in 1996—yet another first for a First Lady. She told millions of prime-time television viewers, "I wish we could be sitting around a kitchen table, just us, talking about our hopes and fears about our children's futures."[279]

To reach even more Americans, Hillary also wrote. Like Eleanor Roosevelt, she published chatty newspaper articles, called "Talking It Over," on balancing family life, work, and friends—that is, how to have it all. In a book titled *Dear Socks, Dear Buddy: Kids' Letters to the First Pets*, she shared mail that children had sent to Chelsea's cat and Bill's Labrador.

She pointed out in a book called *It Takes a Village: And Other Lessons Children Teach Us* that children need support from lots of people in addition to their parents. Teachers, clergy, neighbors, doctors, relatives, and the government all make up a child's village.

Hillary addressed questions she'd been pondering for decades. Can families make it on their own? How much should the government help out, such as by giving poor children free lunches at school or requiring that infants' car seats be safe? Still a heart-liberal, Hillary made the case for federal food programs and safety standards.

- "Home is a child's first and most important classroom."[280]
- "Parents have to back up school authority and quit making excuses for our kids when they misbehave."[281]
- "Knowing what to expect next gives children a sense of security."[282]
- "We must respect the choices that each woman makes for herself and her family."[283]

The book was so popular that Hillary recorded it—and won a Grammy Award for Best Spoken Word Album. When Bill ran for reelection in 1996, however, his Republican opponent, Senator Robert Dole, stated, "I am here to tell you it does not take a village to raise a child. It takes a family to raise a child."[284] Like many Republicans, he believed that it was not the government's job to give families, even needy ones, a helping hand.

Hillary partly agreed with him—and ended up infuriating Democrats. Shortly before the presidential election, Congress passed a law changing the welfare program so that poor families would get less assistance from the federal government. Marian Wright

Edelman, Hillary's friend who headed the Children's Defense Fund, protested that the new system would harm children. Many Democrats urged Bill to veto the law. But Hillary encouraged him to sign it.

Why would Hillary want to do something that might hurt families and children?

She decided that her father was somewhat right, after all. Too many people were relying on government handouts—welfare needed to be reformed. Also, she was afraid that, if Bill didn't go along with the Republicans, he might lose the election. She figured that it was better for the country to live with a mediocre law than with a Republican president. So, she compromised— something she had not done on health care.

Democrats accused the Clintons of doing what was popular rather than what was right. Marian's husband, who worked for Secretary Shalala, resigned. Hillary said the episode was "painful."[285]

Cookies and Toys in Hillaryland

Generally, though, Hillary cared deeply about children and invited them to her home at the White House.

Chelsea's friends, of course, were always welcome. When a key aide had a baby, Hillary had Chelsea's old crib set up in the residence so his grandmother could take care of him nearby.

Speechwriter Lissa Muscatine's twins also loved going to Hillaryland. They knew where the toys, candy, and cookies were stored. The December that they were four years old—when one of the twins was taking ballet lessons—Lissa bought tickets to see *The Nutcracker*. She wanted them to see Chelsea, who had been rehearsing for the production all fall. But Lissa discovered that Chelsea was not scheduled to appear that day. So, Hillary ferried the twins and their mother in the White House limousine to a dress rehearsal in which Chelsea performed. They were enthralled at this very special and personal treat.

Children also attended official events at the White House. Hillary hosted a conference on teenagers where a panel of experts discussed what teens need, such as connections with caring adults. In addition to doctors and psychologists, the experts included actual teenagers.

A twelve-year-old accordion player entertained guests at a state dinner honoring the president of Hungary.

A seventh grader acted out a poem during National Poetry Month. Dozens of kids and their new parents celebrated National Adoption Month at the White House. And thousands trampled the lawn every year for the traditional Easter egg hunt.

Gala Events

Part of Hillary's duties as First Lady involved planning events like Christmas festivities and formal dinners. She made a point of highlighting American food and arts and crafts at these occasions. She enjoyed them so much that she wrote yet another book—*An Invitation to the White House: At Home with History*, which was filled with photographs and recipes.

For her first Christmas in the White House, Hillary chose angels as her theme. She often wore angel pins because she believed they watched over her. The decorations, cards, food, and music, all related to the theme, were planned throughout the year but kept secret until December. Hillary discovered that the job of overseeing the holiday preparations was as demanding as directing a major Broadway show. She also hosted Jewish Chanukah celebrations as well as Eid al-Fitr dinners to observe the end of the Muslim month of Ramadan.

Official visits by heads of foreign governments involved especially complex planning. These occasions were not just social; they were also political. She had to choose dinner guests, menus, table decorations, gifts, and entertainment that the visiting dignitaries would enjoy. After all, the First Lady can't serve a dish that the guest of honor is allergic to. Or seat tablemates together who might get into an argument. A protocol officer and a social secretary oversaw details to make sure everything ran smoothly.

· ·

OFFICIAL VISITS

Protocol ranks visits by dignitaries to the White House according to the level of the visitor and the purpose of the meeting. "State visits" are reserved for a head of state, generally a king, queen, or president. That person is honored with a twenty-one-gun salute. "Official visits" welcome other heads of government, such as a prime minister. They receive nineteen-gun salutes. "Working visits" include meetings with the president and cabinet but do not include arrival ceremonies or state dinners. Other events honor important citizens, such as artists and scientists.

Visiting heads of state stay in Blair House, townhomes across the street from the White House. The staff tries to meet every need; however, some visitors have demanded that guards stand in the nude to be sure they carry no weapons. Others have imported snakes, and their own chefs to cook them.

. . . .

Hillary especially enjoyed the state dinner she and Bill hosted in 1994 for President Nelson Mandela, the first black president of the Republic of South Africa. With nearly two hundred guests, this was one of the largest state dinners ever held at the White House. Two different sets of china were needed. Red cloths draped tables decorated with gilded vases of pale-pink roses and tall candles. Following formal toasts, guests dined on a four-course meal. Afterward, they heard one of Mandela's favorite singers, Whitney Houston, perform in a tent in the Rose Garden. The evening was so special that the television station C-SPAN broadcast the affair.

"Just Bring the Whole Party!"

Perhaps the most elaborate event during Hillary's eight years in the White House was the turn of the millennium, on December 31, 1999. Hillary and Bill invited many of their old friends as well as hundreds of accomplished Americans.

One of her closest buddies, however, almost didn't make it. Jan Piercy's husband had told their eleven-year-old daughter, Lissa, that she could host a sleepover that night. Knowing they'd never find a babysitter, Jan declined the invitation. Hillary responded, "Just bring the whole party!"[286]

"I got to bring my eight best friends to the White House New Year's Eve celebration!" Lissa exclaimed. "We watched the concert on the Mall. Two of my friends were sitting behind Usher."[287]

They didn't sleep much that night. Just before twelve o'clock, five children were asked to light a fuse, which ran the length of the reflecting pool, and, with perfect timing, illuminated the Washington Monument precisely at midnight. As she does every New Year's Eve,

Hillary sang "God Bless America." Music and dancing followed all night long. Some of the musicians were ones whose recordings Hillary had lip-synched to when she was in law school.

"1-9-6-9 Wellesley, Rah!"

Most occasions at the White House were less complex— but still fun. For her twenty-fifth Wellesley College reunion, Hillary invited the entire class. Over three hundred women showed up, from as far away as Togo and Pakistan.

Both the home and the hostess were special. But, for the group, this was just another warm and friendly reunion. One friend admitted, "We were the only people that had ever come to the White House that had rearranged the furniture! That's because we were pulling up chairs to talk to one another."[288]

Just as the classmates did on the chapel steps almost thirty years earlier, they sang. Grace before dinner consisted of "Johnny Appleseed"—"Oh, the Lord is good to me/And so I thank the Lord . . ."

They also chanted their class cheer, sort of. The college administration never approved any that they composed. So, they belted out:

> 1-9-6-9 Wellesley, rah!
> 1-9-6-9 Wellesley.
> Twenty-fifth year, still no cheer!
> 1-9-6-9 Wellesley.

Watching her, Bill said, "Hillary was never happier than when she had her Wellesley classmates around."[289]

Several friends were invited at other times for small lunches and dinners as well. One confessed that she pilfered half a dozen paper hand towels embossed with the presidential seal from a guest powder room. Fortunately, she discovered a supply in a cabinet under the sink to replace the ones she stashed in her purse.

Birthdays, too, were occasions for celebration. Hillary so enjoyed dressing as Dolley Madison that costume parties became a tradition. With each one, she got to try on a different "me,"[290] as she had in college. In 1994, Hillaryland surprised her with a 1950s poodle skirt. Chelsea tied her hair in a ponytail with a chiffon scarf. And Bill sported a black leather jacket and jeans as they jitterbugged the night away.

The observance of Hillary's fiftieth birthday in 1997 continued over five days, beginning with a White House conference on child care. Treats included her mom's meat loaf with dill pickles, PB&J on crustless white bread, and a five-tier cake topped by a frosting image of *It Takes a Village*. The finale entailed a day-long party in Chicago.

She also remembered the birthdays of everyone in Hillaryland. And for Chelsea's sixteenth, teens spent a weekend at the First Family's other home—Camp David—where they played paintball with the Marines stationed there.

Keeping Up Appearances

The White House receives about five thousand visitors every day. Tour guides and other staff greet them but making sure the historic residence remains elegant falls to the First Lady. In addition to the changes she made to the residence for her family's comfort, Hillary over-saw her share of renovations:

- Replacement of a defunct air-conditioning system
- Removal of eleven big game heads, which Theodore Roosevelt had shot, from the state dining room and replacement of the room's draperies and carpeting
- Re-wallpapering of the Blue Room and reupholstering the furniture
- Recovering the Grand Staircase with brilliant red-and-gold carpeting
- Repainting the Map Room and hanging President Roosevelt's World War II maps

All of these redecorating jobs were completed in time for the two-hundredth anniversary of the White House on November 1, 2000. Three former presidents and their wives joined the Clintons for a celebratory dinner.

The White House Minus One

In September 1997, Hillary's home suddenly seemed to become larger, or maybe quieter—certainly emptier. During the previous year, she and Bill had taken

Chelsea to visit colleges. Surely, she would want to go to Wellesley!

Chelsea, however, fell in love with Stanford University in California, which was three thousand miles and three time zones from Washington, DC. Hearing her choice, Hillary blurted, "You can't go that far away."[291] But when the time came, she and Bill took their daughter to her new home and even helped her settle in.

Wielding a small screwdriver, Bill dismantled the bunk beds for Chelsea and her roommate. Hillary lined all of the dresser drawers. The Secret Service installed bulletproof windows. Hillary was sad to leave her daughter behind. Yet she knew that Chelsea was better prepared for college than she had been in 1965.

CHAPTER 9

The White House: Disasters and Decisions
1995-2000

. . . .

"Rummaging Through Our Lives"

Hillary's to-do list as First Lady was endless: reform health care, write books, spend time with Chelsea, redecorate the White House, hold convenings around the world, host dinners, fix welfare. Some of her efforts succeeded; some failed; many were criticized. Yet she kept trying to do all the good she could.

Kenneth Starr, the special prosecutor, meanwhile, had one job. From 1994 to 1998, he searched for a crime.

The Clintons had already been found innocent of wrongdoing in Whitewater, their bad investment in vacation homes in Arkansas. And Hillary had been cleared of having her friend Vince murdered. But Republicans refused to accept these decisions, and in August 1994, they directed Starr to keep looking.

He said he intended to "investigate the facts fully . . ."[292] Hillary feared that he intended "to ruin the lives of public figures"[293]—especially hers.

To gather the facts, Starr demanded copies of the Clintons' business deals. Hillary was infuriated that he was "rummaging through our lives, looking at every check we had written."[294] Starr was suspicious when she claimed she couldn't find her Whitewater paperwork. Then, in January 1996, the records suddenly appeared. After Hillary and her staff searched for two years, an aide found them in her office. Hardly anyone believed Hillary when she explained that they were missing because the third floor of the White House was "a mess."[295] A columnist for the *New York Times* labeled her a "congenital liar."[296]

Starr summoned Hillary to appear before a grand jury, which would decide if there was enough evidence to send her to trial. This was another first for a First Lady, but not one she was happy about. He even had her show up at the courthouse rather than question her at home. Starr wanted "to humiliate me publicly,"[297] she protested.

On January 26, 1996, Hillary wore a boldly embroidered coat to her hearing and waved cheerfully at the press. "I was determined not to let him break my spirit,"[298] she said. After questioning her, the grand jury found no evidence of a crime. Nevertheless, Starr kept hunting for nearly two more years. Finally, in December 1997, he gave up and closed the investigation.

A month later, he reopened it and switched his focus from Hillary's affairs to Bill's.

"I Never Told Anybody to Lie"

Early on the morning of January 21, 1998, Bill nudged Hillary awake.

"You're not going to believe this,"[299] he said.

He wanted to warn her that the *Washington Post* was running a story under the headline "Clinton Accused of Urging Aide to Lie."[300] The article went on to say that he had had an improper relationship with a young intern at the White House named Monica Lewinsky.

Hillary knew that Bill had had inappropriate relationships with other women before. But he told her that this article was false. He had not told Monica to lie because there was nothing to lie about.

Bill guessed right: Hillary didn't believe the news story. She believed him. The accusation about Bill and Monica, she thought, "seemed like just another vicious scandal manufactured by political opponents."[301] Since they couldn't defeat him in elections, they were smearing his reputation.

In a television interview several days later, Hillary blamed a "vast right-wing conspiracy"[302] for the false charges. Bill, too, went on television to denounce them. "I never told anybody to lie," he stated, "not a single time. Never."[303]

Knowing that Chelsea would be worried, they called her at Stanford. Hillary assured her, "These people are telling lies." She reminded her daughter, "You have heard this all your life."[304] Bill told everyone—the American people, his cabinet secretaries, lawyers, staff, and friends—that he had not behaved improperly.

Bill's denials didn't convince Ken Starr, however. For the next seven months, he questioned Bill, interviewed witnesses, and gathered evidence. Hillary's prediction that a special prosecutor could look into everything, forever, was coming to pass.

Even worse, he didn't follow the rules for secrecy that John Doar, who had led the investigation of President Nixon, required. Starr's findings appeared in the news. Someone must have leaked them, illegally, to the press. The First Couple was furious.

Republicans began to clamor for the president to resign.

"Never!"[305] exclaimed Bill. Resigning would be preposterous, Hillary agreed, since he hadn't done anything wrong.

The constant news stories and attacks made it hard to accomplish much work. A White House staffer said, "The personal piece was hard enough for her. The political piece was really challenging as well."[306]

Personal Challenges: "I'm Sorry. I'm So Sorry."

Early on the morning of August 15, 1998, Bill again nudged Hillary awake—just as he had done in January. This time, however, he told her the truth: he *had* had an inappropriate relationship with Monica.

Sobbing, Hillary yelled, "Why did you lie to me?"[307]

He explained that he knew she would be hurt and angry if he told her. So, instead, he claimed that the news reports about himself and Monica were false. He was admitting it now because Starr had uncovered the facts and insisted that Bill testify before a grand jury.

Hillary was "dumbfounded, heartbroken, and outraged"[308] at her husband's behavior. She had believed him!

"I'm sorry. I'm so sorry," Bill repeated over and over.

She told him he also had to apologize to Chelsea, who was home for summer vacation. He wept. Like her mother, Chelsea was confused and hurt. Two days later, Bill confessed on television to the American people.

The special prosecutor, however, would not accept a mere apology. Starr had asked Bill about his relationship with Monica eight months earlier. Even though Bill had sworn an oath to tell the truth, he misled—possibly even lied to—Starr. As a result, the president could be impeached. If he lost, Bill would be the first president to be kicked out of the White House.

Either way, Hillary had to consider whether or not to stay married to him.

"I Felt Unbearably Lonely"

Almost every family experiences difficult times—physical or emotional illness, for example, or financial problems. When these difficulties occur, most couples figure out what to do in private. Hillary and Bill didn't have that opportunity. Every misstep, disagreement, or accusation quickly became public. As a result, they had to deal with themselves, each other, Chelsea, the press, and the public all at once.

"I didn't know whether our marriage could—or should—survive," Hillary said. "This was the most devastating, shocking, and hurtful experience of my life."[309]

Chelsea did her best to either keep her parents together or keep them apart. When the First Family headed for a vacation on Martha's Vineyard, Massachusetts, in late August, she walked between them, holding hands with both, while they seemed to veer in opposite directions.

Hillary Rodham in her Easter dress, 1960.
(Clinton Presidential Library; Clinton Family Collection)

Laura Grosch paints Hillary's face at a be-in, 1967.
(Photo by Dana Semeraro, from Laura Grosch's personal collection)

Hillary and Bill Clinton in Yale moot court with their classmates, January 1973.
(Clinton Presidential Library; Clinton Family Collection)

Hillary and Bill on their wedding day, October 11, 1975.
(Clinton Presidential Library; Clinton Family Collection)

Hillary and Bill holding baby Chelsea, March 4, 1980.
(Clinton Presidential Library; Clinton Family Collection)

Hillary, Bill, and Chelsea celebrating at the 1992
Democratic National Convention.
(Clinton Presidential Library; Clinton Family Collection)

Hillary dressed as Dolley Madison and Bill Clinton dressed as James Madison at Hillary's birthday celebration and costume party, October 26, 1993. *(Clinton Presidential Library)*

Hillary speaks about health-care reform on March 14, 1994, at the University of Colorado Boulder. *(Clinton Presidential Library)*

As First Lady, Hillary unveils the renovated Blue Room
of the White House, February 17, 1995. *(AP Photo/J. Scott Applewhite)*

Hillary speaks at the Fourth United Nations World Conference
on Women in Beijing, China, September 5, 1995.
(Clinton Presidential Library)

Hillary and her daughter, Chelsea, with children at the orphanage run by Christian missionary Mother Teresa in New Delhi on March 28, 1995, during a twelve-day goodwill tour of South Asia. *(Reuters/Win McNamee)*

President Clinton, daughter Chelsea, and First Lady Hillary Rodham Clinton walk with their Labrador, Buddy, to board Marine One on the South Lawn of the White House, August 18, 1998, the day after the president admitted to an inappropriate relationship with an intern. *(AP Photo/J. Scott Applewhite)*

Hillary is sworn in as senator from New York, January 3, 2001. *(Clinton Presidential Library)*

Democratic presidential hopeful Senator Hillary Rodham Clinton
(D-NY), left, answers a question as Senator Barack Obama (D-IL),
center, and former Senator John Edwards (D-NC), listen during a
Democratic presidential debate in Myrtle Beach, South Carolina,
January 21, 2008. *(AP Photo/Mary Ann Chastain)*

Texts from Hillary: As US secretary of state, Hillary checks her
electronic device while in a military C-17 plane bound for Tripoli,
Libya, October 18, 2011. *(Reuters/Kevin Lamarque)*

A group of Hillary's friends rallied to greet her at the airport. She took long walks on the beach, sometimes alone, sometimes with other women. Mostly, she read and prayed.

Back at the White House, Betsy Johnson Ebeling, her old friend from Park Ridge, came to visit, along with another friend from Little Rock. They noticed that she wasn't speaking to Bill. She couldn't talk with them, either, about her troubles. Everything was public but, at the same time, felt too private to share. In any case, her lawyers told her she couldn't talk to anyone but them.

"I felt unbearably lonely,"[310] Hillary said.

. . . .

GLAMOROUS DISTRACTIONS

Hillary found distractions even during this lonely time. The singer Stevie Wonder composed a song just for her and came to the White House to perform it. She felt consoled as he sang and played "No One Walks On Water," about the importance of forgiveness.

Then, *Vogue*, a fashion magazine, did a photo shoot of Hillary dressed in a glamorous gown. "I escaped into a world of makeup artists . . . giving me the chance to look good when I had been feeling so low,"[311] she said. The article was titled "The Extraordinary Hillary Clinton."[312]

. . . .

"Grace?"

While making up her mind about her marriage, she pondered several factors.

"My long hours alone made me admit to myself that I loved him,"[313] she realized. Still, that did not necessarily mean she should continue to live with Bill.

Hillary also had to think about what was best for Chelsea, even though her daughter was already in college. A Wellesley friend advised Hillary to leave Bill because his behavior was not good for the teenager. However, she had written in *It Takes a Village*, "children without fathers, or whose parents float in and out of their lives after divorce, are precarious little boats in the most turbulent seas."[314] Surely Chelsea didn't need more storms in her life. Yet which way would her life be calmer—with or without her father?

Dorothy Rodham no longer told her daughter what to do. On the other hand, Hillary might have recalled the lesson her mother taught her: *"You do not leave the marriage."*[315] Was Dorothy's decision to stay with Hugh the right one for Hillary?

In addition to a marriage counselor, the other person Hillary knew she could count on for wise guidance was Don Jones. Her youth minister reminded her of a sermon he had read to the group in Park Ridge thirty-five years earlier. Written by a philosopher named Paul Tillich, it was titled "You Are Accepted." The sermon explained Methodists' view of "grace."

"Grace strikes us when we are in great pain," Tillich wrote. Hillary was certainly in pain. He continued, "Sometimes at that moment, a wave of light breaks into our darkness, and it is as though a voice were saying: 'You are accepted.' . . . If that happens to us, we experience grace."

Hillary understood that she could not hunt for grace the way Starr searched for a crime. According to Methodist belief, "It happens; or it does not happen."[316] She also knew that God would forgive Bill, no matter what he did.

So, reading Scripture and her scrapbook of prayers, she waited for grace. If it happened, perhaps she could forgive and accept him as he was too.

Political Challenges: "Grounds to Impeach?"

Ken Starr did not wait patiently. He intended to see Bill Clinton impeached as soon as possible. Hillary believed Starr hoped for that even before he found reasons to do so. Yet, based on her experience investigating President Nixon, she did not believe that the reasons existed.

"There were no grounds to impeach Bill,"[317] Hillary argued. He had behaved badly, but he had not committed any high crimes or misdemeanors.

Starr disagreed. Here's what happened.

SEPTEMBER 9, 1998: Special Prosecutor Ken Starr delivered the report on his investigation of Bill Clinton to the House of Representatives. It cited eleven crimes for which the president could be impeached.

OCTOBER 8, 1998: The House of Representatives,

including thirty-one Democrats, voted to impeach the president.

NOVEMBER–DECEMBER 1998: The Judiciary Committee held hearings, and on December 11–12, it approved four articles (reasons) to impeach the president.

DECEMBER 19, 1998: The House of Representatives approved two articles of impeachment—perjury (for lying under oath) and obstruction of justice.

JANUARY 7, 1999: With Supreme Court Chief Justice William Rehnquist presiding, the Senate tried President Clinton.

FEBRUARY 12, 1999: The Senate acquitted the president of both charges.

The US Senate agreed with Hillary: Bill was not guilty.

Personal and Political: "We Just Have a Deep Connection"

Before the Senate reached this verdict, Hillary worked behind the scenes to convince Congress that Bill was innocent. She met with Democratic congresswomen and urged them to support him. She told other congressional leaders, "You all may be mad at Bill Clinton. Certainly, I'm not happy about what my husband did. But impeachment is not the answer."[318]

Why would she defend him after he lied to her? Hillary realized that "he was not only my husband, he was also my president."[319] And she respected the way he led America. Hillary felt hurt personally but she supported Bill politically.

The Senate's impeachment trial lasted an excruciating five weeks. Hillary and Bill did not know how it would end—whether he would remain the president or whether Vice President Al Gore would replace him.

"I was relying more on my faith every day," she said. To stay optimistic, she recalled the definition she had learned in Sunday school. "Faith is like stepping off a cliff and expecting one of two outcomes—you will either land on solid ground or you will be taught to fly."[320]

During that time—late 1998 and early 1999— prayer and counseling helped Hillary decide to stand by her man not only politically but also personally. He admitted what he'd done and asked for forgiveness, and, eventually, she forgave him.

"We just have a deep connection that transcends whatever happens,"[321] she realized.

Hillary was relieved that she and Bill could return to being the First Couple. But she knew that she was not satisfied remaining only the First Lady.

"I'd Like to Be On the Inside"

"A lot of people think when you leave the White House, you ought to run for US senator from New York!"[322]

An acquaintance from Arkansas said this to Hillary at a holiday party in December 1997. The Christmas theme that year was "Santa's Workshop." Standing near a tree that shimmered with sparkling lights and elves crafting miniature rocking horses, Hillary responded, "You're kidding!" Then she belted out her famous guffaw.

The next year, Democratic leaders in Congress made the same plea—for good reason. A poll on New Year's Eve 1998 named Hillary the most admired woman in America. Furthermore, Senator Moynihan had recently announced his retirement; his seat would be empty. She insisted she wasn't interested.

Hillaryland, however, knew that behind closed doors, she was seriously considering running for the Senate. Her staff was opposed. One close aide said the idea was "kooky."[323] Others said she would lose the election.

If Hillary had made a list of reasons for and against a Senate campaign during this time, it might have looked like this.

Pros

- A lot of New Yorkers must like me, since they're urging me to run.
- Bill is so popular, he could campaign and help me win.
- I need a job.

Cons

- I've never lived in New York. I'm not even registered to vote there. Voters will accuse me of being a "carpetbagger," an outsider who takes control.
- I haven't run for office since 1968 at Wellesley. And I'd have to campaign while serving as First Lady.

- Republicans would go after me. The campaign would be nasty and could cost as much as twenty-five million dollars!
- My opponent, New York City's Mayor Rudy Giuliani, is tough. Hillaryland predicts he'd win.
- My jobs right now are to keep Bill from getting impeached and to decide whether or not to stay married to him.
- Instead of being a senator, I could run a foundation or corporation, become a college president, or host a television show.
- Being a senator from New York is an impossible job. The state covers fifty-four thousand square miles and contains everything from rural dairy farms to poor mill towns to the eight million people in New York City.
- If I somehow won, I'd have to get along with those Republican senators who voted against my health reform legislation and who might vote to impeach Bill.
- Bill is so popular, he could outshine me when we campaign together.

It certainly looked as if the cons won. Many people thought—and hoped—so. Hillary remained undecided but she did not deny rumors that she might go for it.

"I needed a push,"[324] she said. That push came from a teenager in New York.

In March 1999, Hillary attended an event honoring female athletes at a high school. Above the stage hung a banner with the words "Dare to Compete." The captain of the girls' basketball team cleverly introduced Hillary—the former tomboy—as "a runner"[325] and whispered in her ear, "Dare to compete, Mrs. Clinton."[326]

That impertinent but inspiring prod reminded Hillary of a line in one of her favorite movies, *A League of Their Own*, about a women's baseball team. The demanding coach tells a player who wants to quit, "If it wasn't hard, everyone would do it—the hard is what makes it great."[327]

Hillary had never shrunk from daunting challenges. In fact, she seemed drawn to them, the way climbers are to Mount Everest.

In June that year, Hillary hosted the thirtieth reunion

of the Wellesley College Class of '69 at the White House. Toward the end of the evening, she asked Jan Piercy and Alan Schechter, her friend and her professor, to join her in the solarium. They listened as she explained the "crazy thing I'm contemplating."[328] In fact, although she had not yet announced it, she had made her decision.

"I have lobbied Congress," she told them. "I have been standing outside, knocking on the door, while they set policy and pass laws. I'd like to be on the inside."[329]

While working on health care, Hillary had tried to wield power from the West Wing of the White House. But she had failed. The power she wanted now resided in Congress.

Jan wasn't surprised. "She did not want to go down in history as First Lady,"[330] Jan said. Hillary wanted to make history in her own right.

"You Restored My Faith in My Government"

In July 1999, Hillary launched a listening tour of New York. Just as she had asked her classmates for their opinions when she ran for college government, she wanted to hear what the state's citizens wanted from their leaders. And just as she had visited every county in Arkansas while working on education reform, her Senate tour took her to all sixty-two counties in New York.

Kitchen-table issues were on everyone's minds. Parents in big cities yearned for smaller classes and better after-school programs for their children. Upstate dairy farmers wanted to raise the price of milk. A woman concerned that young people couldn't find jobs was impressed. "She's actually listening to what you're saying,"[331] she said.

On February 6, 2000, Hillary announced her candidacy in the gym at the State University of New York at Purchase. Referring to her Wellesley graduation speech, she told two thousand supporters, "Politics is the art of making possible what seems to be impossible, and that is why I want to be your senator."[332] The crowd cheered.

Standing with her were the state's two senators—Daniel Patrick Moynihan and Charles Schumer—both of whom praised her. In between them, a fifteen-year-old girl also spoke.

Amity Weiss, who had won *Seventeen* magazine's Volunteerism Award the year before, read a letter she had written to Hillary after hearing her on the tour.

"You spoke of democracy and how vital it is to the world. You spoke of how important participation in government and the political process are in making our democracy work," Amity said. "You restored my faith in my government."[333]

With that, "Hillary," as her campaign buttons and yard signs called her, was off and running—for US senator from the state of New York.

"The most difficult decisions I have made in my life were to stay married to Bill and to run for the Senate from New York,"[334] she said. She made these decisions within months of each other. As for Bill, she moved from hurt to forgiveness. With regard to the Senate, she hoped to move from behind-the-scenes influence at the White House to voting membership in Congress.

CHAPTER 10

Senator Hillary
2000–2008

. . . .

"A New Democrat"

Hillary's first job as a candidate for the US Senate wasn't to run for office. Before she could do that, she had to settle down—in New York. Otherwise, she wouldn't be able to represent the state. She and Bill bought a century-old Colonial-style home in Chappaqua, a small town thirty-five miles north of New York City. The eleven-room home, the first place they could call their own in almost twenty years, was located on a street appropriately named Old House Lane. Now she was officially a resident.

Planning her campaign, Hillary recalled messages

she had heard during her listening tour. Questions about how much the government should do—for dairy farmers and schoolchildren, for instance—continued to swirl. She decided to take a middle road.

Calling herself a "new Democrat," Hillary said, "I don't believe that government is the source of all our problems or the solution to them. But I do believe that when people live up to their responsibilities, we ought to live up to ours, to help them build better lives."[335] That is, help people who help themselves.

With this message, she spent much of the year traveling around her adopted state. Hillary had campaigned frequently with Bill but never for herself. Supporters waved placards reading "Welcome, Hillary!" Other signs ordered her to "Go home." These implied that she was a carpetbagger, like the Northerners who moved to the South after the Civil War to seize power from the locals. Uncomfortable shaking hundreds of hands every day, she said, "I'm a baby campaigner."[336] But she got used to the crowds and even talked with the press.

Hillary also sometimes spent the night in people's homes so they could get to know her the way her friends and Hillaryland did. In the morning, she stripped the sheets off her bed and cleared the breakfast table.

Over school vacations, Chelsea took her mother's place hosting events at the White House and joined her father on official trips to Colombia, Japan, and New Zealand. In the fall, she took a leave of absence from Stanford to help with the campaign. Chelsea also cast her first-ever vote, for her mom.

On November 7, 2000, Hillary soundly defeated her opponent, Congressman Rick Lazio, who had replaced Giuliani, 55 percent to 43 percent. Hillary would no longer be just "the former First Lady." She had been reaching for higher positions since running for head of college government at Wellesley. Now, grabbing the next ring on the crossbars, she would soon be "Senator Clinton"— a feat no other president's spouse had achieved.

Freshmen senators receive a tour of the Capitol and orientation on that body's rules. The night before Hillary's, Bill kidded her "about going to her first day of 'Senator School.'" He told her she had to "get a good night's sleep and wear a nice outfit."[337] He even joked about sprinting after her limousine with her brown-bag lunch in his hand.

On January 3, 2001, Hillary walked onto the Senate

floor and was sworn into office as a member of the 107th Congress. Only a dozen other senators were women, and they all topped their outfits with a jacket, as required by the chamber's rules. Bill, Chelsea, and Dorothy, who were not allowed in the chamber, watched from the visitors' gallery.

Separately, Hillary held a mock ceremony to involve her family. "After I held the Bible for all of Bill's swearing-in ceremonies," Hillary said, "he and Chelsea held the Bible for me."[338]

For the final seventeen days of Bill's presidency, the First Couple was the first to serve in both the White House and Congress. On Inauguration Day, Hillary and Bill moved out of their home of the last eight tumultuous years and into another new home they bought in the quiet Embassy Row area of Washington. They called this one, a three-story Georgian like many residences in Park Ridge and Wellesley, Whitehaven. Dorothy moved in with them.

· ·

MOVING DAY

Moving out of the White House was even more hectic than moving in. Over eight years,

Hillary had acquired a large wardrobe, and Bill had received thousands of gifts. Official presents from foreign heads of state had to be separated from personal items and shipped to the Clinton Library in Little Rock, Arkansas.

On January 20, 2001—the day that incoming President George W. Bush was inaugurated—a Marine Band escorted the departing First Couple through the Grand Foyer. A White House usher led Hillary in a spontaneous waltz until Bill cut in for the final dance.

. . . .

Hillary also moved into her first real office since her days as a working lawyer in Little Rock. Although she and her staff were initially housed in a cramped and windowless basement storage space, she soon moved into Moynihan's area—Suite 476 of the Russell Senate Office Building. Repainted her favorite color—daffodil yellow—her spacious headquarters displayed needlepoint pillows stitched with "It Takes a Village" and "Senator Hillary." A mock photograph showed her sitting with her heroine, Eleanor Roosevelt.

"The Hill," as she was known in college, was on the Hill! And, she reported, she was ecstatic to "continue the work I have been doing for over thirty years on behalf of children and families."[339]

"Be a Workhorse"

From the outside, the United States Senate seems like the lunch table in the cafeteria where the cool kids sit. Called "the world's most exclusive club,"[340] the Senate even has its own dining room.

To join the club, its members—limited to a total of one hundred—have to win a popularity contest. Most of them are rich—in fact, millionaires. And (with the help of the House of Representatives) they make the laws.

On the inside, though, the Senate has cliques and bullies, like any school. When Hillary entered as the new kid, some of the upperclassmen wanted to play rough. One of them, Trent Lott, the Republican Majority Leader from Mississippi, stated, "She will be one of a hundred, and we won't let her forget it."[341]

Hillary didn't punch them out, however, as she had punched Suzy, her neighbor in Park Ridge. Not even the senators who had killed her health reform bill or voted to impeach her husband. Instead, she made friends with them.

• •

"OH NO!"

A senator's first speech in the chamber, called the "maiden speech," is a noteworthy occasion. Members choose a topic that is important to them and invite family members to listen in the visitors' gallery or watch on television. Hillary gave a talk on health care. Leaving the chamber afterward, she abruptly halted and exclaimed, "Oh no!" Ann O'Leary, her deputy chief of staff, who had come to congratulate her, wondered what was wrong. "I forgot to call my mother to tell her to turn on C-SPAN!" Hillary said. "My mom's going to be so disappointed. She didn't get to watch it live."[342]

The incident reminded Ann that Hillary was "a famous woman doing very important things, but she's also a daughter."[343]

• •

First, she asked Virginia's Senator Robert C. Byrd, an elder statesman who had opposed her health plan, for advice on how to be a good senator. He was flattered by her question and told her, "Be a workhorse, not a show horse."[344]

She understood that, although her fame had helped her win the election, she couldn't act like a superstar. She took Byrd's advice. Like the good student she'd always been, Hillary stayed up late doing her homework for the next day's meetings, woke up early to read the news, and was hardly ever absent when the Senate voted. Byrd said that, of the four hundred senators he'd served with during nearly fifty years there, Hillary was one of his favorites.

• •

HILLARYLAND AT THE SENATE

Hillaryland worked as hard as their boss, often staying late without complaining. One night, however, Ann O'Leary didn't respond when the Senator asked her to attend a meeting.

Hillary said, "I have a feeling you have something else planned." Ann apologized and admitted that she had a date to meet her boyfriend's parents. "Oh my gosh," Hillary replied. "That's so much more important than anything I'm doing . . . You definitely need to go to that!"[345] Years later, after Ann and her boyfriend married and moved away, Hillary called to congratulate them on the birth of their first baby.

. . . .

Hillary also joined the Wednesday prayer group called the Fellowship. One morning, several months into her term, Kansas senator Sam Brownback, who had voted to impeach Bill, spoke up. He confessed that he had hated Hillary and said nasty things about her. But now he saw that she, too, was a person of faith. He turned to her and asked, "Mrs. Clinton, will you forgive me?" She did.

"She reached out to colleagues on both sides of the aisle, including some Republicans who had voted to impeach the president," her former speechwriter Lissa Muscatine said. "That surprised and endeared her to a lot of people."[346]

When she was in the White House, Hillary had tried to work with the Senate but sometimes failed. Now, she was working *within* the Senate. To do so, she crossed the aisle from the Democratic side to the Republican side and sponsored legislation with her former enemies.

"She believed it was essential to come together on legislation affecting the issues she cared about," Lissa explained, "and she was willing to work with anyone in any party to get important bills passed."[347]

For instance, Hillary and Brownback jointly proposed a bill to study how violent video games affect children. She also worked with a conservative member of the House of Representatives on legislation that encouraged couples to adopt older children. She partied across the aisle, too, throwing a bipartisan shower for a female Republican senator who had just adopted a baby. Hillary's wide circle of friendships became essential the very next day, when New York City came under attack.

9/11/2001

September 11 opened bright and clear. Senator Clinton faced a busy day and got right to work—until everything changed.

8:45 A.M.: Hillary left Whitehaven for a meeting on a major education reform bill called No Child Left Behind. She wanted to be sure the bill included items that parents had brought up during her listening tour, like small classes and trained teachers.

8:48 A.M.: Just before she climbed into the backseat of the Suburban for the drive to her office, Hillary learned that a plane had crashed into the north tower of the World Trade Center, a pair of skyscrapers in New York City. What a "terrible accident,"[348] she thought.

9:05 A.M.: Listening to the radio in the car, Hillary heard that a second plane had crashed, this time into the south tower.

9:05:01 A.M.: This was not an accident, she realized. Her next thought was, Is Chelsea safe?

Chelsea was working in New York City, before heading off to graduate school in England. Hillary knew she was planning to jog through a park just three-quarters of a mile from the World Trade Center, then stop near the twin towers for coffee. She frantically called her daughter's cell phone. No answer. New York City's networks were down.

Hillary also called Bill in Australia, where it was midnight. He was hopelessly far away, so she assured him Chelsea was fine.

9:30 A.M.: Hillary arrived at her office and watched the havoc in New York on television. The city, she said, looked wounded.

9:37 A.M.: Reporters announced the crash of a third plane—into the Pentagon, just outside Washington. Hillary was horrified. Still no news of Chelsea.

9:43 A.M.: Senators, including Hillary and her staff, were evacuated to Capitol Police headquarters, several blocks from her office. They were alerted that a fourth plane had been hijacked and was also heading toward Washington. What was happening?

10:00 A.M.: Chelsea called! She'd decided not to jog that morning but had to search for a pay phone. She told her mother it seemed as if the world was falling down around her. It seemed that way to others, too, when the towers actually fell, minutes later.

Chelsea was shaken but fine. The city and the country Hillary represented were not. Almost three thousand people were killed.

"That September morning changed me and what I had to do as a senator, a New Yorker, and an American,"[349] Hillary said.

That evening, several hundred congressmen and women gathered on the steps of the US Capitol. After a moment of silence in memory of the day's victims, they sang "God Bless America"—the same tune Hillary sang every New Year's Eve. Her eyes teared up.

Tougher on the Senate floor the next day, she condemned the "attack on America."[350] She also pledged to support President Bush. Hillary disagreed with him on many issues. Nevertheless, she believed it was important to back the president in case America went to war.

All air traffic across America was halted. But Hillary and Senator Schumer flew in a helicopter over Ground Zero, the pile of debris where the towers once stood.

"Smoke was still rising from the smoldering wreckage," she said. "I could see twisted girders and shattered beams looming above the first responders."[351] These were the firemen, police, construction workers, medical teams, volunteers, and others who rushed to search for survivors and clear the site.

When the senators landed, they discovered that the situation was even worse on the ground. "The air was acrid, and the thick smoke made it hard to breathe or see," Hillary noticed. "I was wearing a surgical mask, but the air burned my throat and lungs."[352]

Back in Washington, she called on Senator Byrd. He chaired the Appropriations Committee, which decides how federal funds should be spent.

"We're in real trouble, and it's going to take a lot to put the city back together. Can you help?"[353] she pleaded.

"Think of me as the third senator from New York,"[354] Byrd responded. With support from a man who had formerly opposed her, Hillary and Schumer got $20 billion for their state's largest city.

She also helped persuade the president to double the amount of money he offered to rebuild New York.

Despite their differences of opinion, Hillary and Bush stood atop the rubble at Ground Zero, symbolizing America coming together.

Responders labored on "the Pile" for months. She worried that they would develop lung problems from breathing in dangerous particles. Cleverly, she used her power as a member of the Senate Committee on Environment and Public Works to obtain even more money to treat the workers—70 percent of whom did get sick.

Over time, Hillary also helped create the September 11 Victim Compensation Fund, which paid for survivors' long-term medical needs. In addition, she helped found the 9/11 Commission, which studied the attacks and those who committed them—a terrorist organization called al Qaeda, led by Osama bin Laden.

"A Grave Threat"?

"I want to discuss a grave threat to peace," President Bush told Americans a year after 9/11. "The threat comes from Iraq."[355]

Bin Laden operated from several countries—though not Iraq. Nevertheless, Bush believed that this country and its president, Saddam Hussein, supported the terrorist leader and his organization. Bush also believed that Hussein was making weapons of mass destruction, such as poisonous gases, and was developing nuclear bombs. These could kill millions of people. The United Nations tried to inspect the weapons but Hussein refused, insisting he didn't have them.

President Bush asked Congress to allow him to declare war on Iraq if the UN's efforts failed. Hillary had promised to support the president, so she voted "yea." However, this time, she had not finished her homework.

A top-secret government report showed that Hussein might have been telling the truth. He probably did not stockpile weapons of mass destruction, definitely did not support al Qaeda or bin Laden, and was nowhere near creating a nuclear bomb. There was not a strong reason to attack Iraq. And doing so would not protect America from terrorists.

It appears that Hillary did not read the report. She claimed she was briefed on it; however, the research contradicted her statement.

"The facts that have brought us to this fateful vote are

not in doubt," she asserted. "Saddam Hussein . . . has given aid, comfort, and sanctuary to terrorists, including al Qaeda members."[356] She urged the president to find another solution besides invading Iraq—then voted to allow him to declare war. In March 2003, he did.

Hillary gave several reasons for her decision. Above all, she wanted to stand by her president, combat terrorism, and support the women and men of America's armed services. So she cast her vote for war "with conviction."[357]

Many people believed she also wanted to prove that she could be tough. In the fall of 2006, she would have to run for reelection. New Yorkers, especially those who had survived 9/11, would not want a wimpy senator. There were also rumors that she might seek an even higher office. The first woman president would need to stand for more than just kitchen-table issues. So she might have voted in favor of war with a political strategy in mind as well.

The strategy quickly worked for her but not for the country. In 2003, Hillary was appointed to the powerful Senate Armed Services Committee, which oversees the US military and the Department of Defense. This position allowed her to keep open a military base near Niagara Falls. Saving the base guaranteed jobs for her constituents. In addition, she learned about warfare and demonstrated, again, that a woman could be a "hawk," just as she had been in high school.

This was a busy year for Hillary. She published another book—a memoir titled *Living History*. More than three million copies were sold!

Because of these successes, Hillary won reelection to the Senate in 2006, with an overwhelming 67 percent of the vote. She had transformed herself into a popular and powerful senator—though she was only one of a hundred, she stood out.

Meanwhile, however, thousands of American soldiers and Iraqi soldiers and civilians were being killed and maimed in battle. The US was also involved in an unpopular war in Afghanistan. When Americans learned that Hussein did not have weapons of mass destruction and did not support al Qaeda, many turned against the war, just as Hillary had opposed the Vietnam War in college. They criticized her and other members of Congress who had given Bush the go-ahead. In response, she blamed the president for misleading Congress and mishandling the war.

Hillary knew that if she were president, she would manage better. Ever since college, friends had predicted and hoped that she'd run. In January 2007, she decided to reach for the next ring dangling from the crossbars.

WHAT IF?

In 2004, Katie Couric, a television news journalist, asked Hillary a series of questions about herself. Here's a summary:

KC: "If I weren't a politician, I would be . . . ?"

HRC: "A teacher."

KC: "The thing I hate the most about myself is . . . ?"

HRC: "My impatience . . . I have to take some deep breaths, and just accept things the way they are."

KC: "My guiltiest pleasure is . . . ?"

HRC: "Chocolate. Any kind, anytime, anywhere."

KC: "I'm proudest that . . ."

HRC: "I raised a wonderful daughter."

KC: "I would like my tombstone to say . . . ?"

HRC: "She did her best to live every day to the fullest."[358]

CHAPTER 11

Hillary for President!
2007–2008

. . . .

"I'm In. And I'm In to Win."

Sitting on a plump, floral-print couch in her pale-yellow sunroom at Whitehaven, Hillary looked intently into a video camera. The lens panned past family photos and a vase of pink blossoms as she announced, "I'm starting a campaign" for president of the United States. To do so, she wanted to open "a conversation—with you, with America."[359]

Hillary had conducted a statewide listening tour before her first Senate race. Now, running for the nation's top office, she wanted to hear from citizens around the country. Many of the issues remained the same—good schools, jobs that pay enough for workers to live on, and health care for everyone. But there was also a new one—the war in Iraq. And instead of going on the road right away, Hillary went high tech.

On January 20, 2007—two years to the day before the inauguration of the next president—she posted a video online. She talked with Americans through a series of web chats. She also sent out a mass email stating, "I'm in. And I'm in to win."[360]

In its first five days, more than 140,000 supporters signed up at www.hillaryclinton.com. Her web chats drew fifty thousand viewers. Hillary reached out, as she had been doing since college, but in up-to-the-minute ways. A modern campaign would be important because her major opponent was a young African-American senator named Barack Obama, from her home state of Illinois. She needed to make sure he didn't attract too many young or black voters.

· ·

RULES FOR RUNNING FOR PRESIDENT

To run for president, candidates must file two documents with the Federal Election Commission (FEC). One is a Statement of

Organization, which creates a federal campaign committee. The other is a Statement of Candidacy, which names the candidate and the office being sought. Once these papers are filed, the candidate must follow federal laws that limit campaign contributions and must send records of the amount of money she or he raises and spends.

Before filing with the FEC, many people first establish an exploratory committee. This group helps them decide whether or not to run for office by testing their popularity and predicting how much money they can expect to raise.

. . . .

Running for president is not only a team sport. It's also a math problem—a complicated one with lots of steps and unknowns that can take more than a year to solve. This math puzzle differs from most, however, in a couple of ways. Everyone knows the right answer from the beginning. Yet only one person can get it. Here's the challenge:

- To become the Democratic Party's nominee for president, a candidate must win a majority of the votes from about 4,235 delegates who go to the national convention. A majority is 2,118 people. That's the answer. Strategy is the key to reaching it.

- Over 3,400 of the delegates come from the fifty states (and other areas, such as the District of Columbia and Puerto Rico). The party in each state chooses them by holding either primaries (elections) or caucuses (meetings) or both.

- The delegates promise to vote at the convention for the candidate who wins. Some states split the delegates, according to the results of the primary. Other states require all of them to vote for the winner, even if the election is close.

- The remaining 825 or so are called superdelegates. They're politicians from around the country, and they can vote for whomever they want at the convention.

- The primaries and caucuses are held over about a six-month period, from January to June, in presidential election years. The convention is held that summer or fall. The goal is to win at least 2,118 delegates before the convention starts. May the best candidate win!

This was the task Hillary and her opponents faced in January 2007. But she and her Hillaryland team felt confident that she would win enough primaries to have the nomination sewn up in just over a year. After all, she was one of the most famous people in the world, while hardly anyone had ever heard of the other candidates. Supporters were already giving her campaign money. And, because she had both lived in the White House and served as a senator, she believed she was the most qualified.

Iowa would kick off the campaign season with caucuses in January 2008. Within a month after that, another twenty states would hold primaries. There was no reason for Hillary to think she wouldn't win most of these. With a tailwind of successes giving her momentum, she'd continue to collect delegates from states holding primaries later that spring. Then she'd sail into the Democratic National Convention at the end of August with the nomination in hand.

Her confidence in this game plan didn't mean that Hillary didn't work hard. She spent much of 2007 giving talks, raising money, setting up campaign offices, and rallying supporters. She raised nearly $100 million—surely enough to pay for staff, ads, travel (some by private "Hill-A-Copter"[361]), opinion surveys, and bumper stickers for the next year. Her ratings in popularity polls were high.

Yet by the fall of 2007, she started to stumble over two hurdles. One was Iraq. The other was Obama.

A voter in New Hampshire confronted her. "I want to know if right here, right now, once and for all . . . you can say that war authorization was a mistake."[362] He and many other Democrats wanted Hillary to admit that she should not have voted to allow President Bush to declare war on Iraq.

Although she had begun to regret that decision, she was not ready to say she had been wrong. Republicans would hound her if she confessed to an error. She needed to appear firm, she believed, not flip-floppy, in her decisions.

Some of her supporters, however, began to lean toward Obama. He was not yet a senator when the vote on Iraq was taken but he had spoken out against the war. Many Democrats liked that. They also responded to his message, "Change You Can Believe In." Volunteers signed up in droves to hand out flyers, ferry voters to the polls, and hold fund-raisers. Even people who had little money to spare donated to his campaign, and he raised more than she did.

Worried, Hillary began to attack him. In a televised presidential debate, they argued bitterly, accusing each other of ignoring the needs of poor people. In another debate, she failed to take a position on the war—or on any other issue. Sometimes it seemed that she said whatever she thought was popular—and, at other times, nothing at all. Viewers complained that they didn't know what she stood for.

. . . .

SELMA

On March 7, 2008, Hillary and Obama appeared together in Selma, Alabama. They went there to observe the forty-second anniversary of "Bloody Sunday." This was the day on which state troopers beat black protesters who were marching for the right to vote.

Hillary gave a sermon at a church where she quoted from the speech she heard Dr. Martin Luther King, Jr. give when she was in high school. "We've got to stay awake," she proclaimed, "because we have a march to finish, a march towards one America."[363]

The candidates and churchgoers linked arms and marched, singing "We Shall Overcome."

. . . .

Trying to defend his wife, Bill got into the act. In one of his speeches, he seemed to say that Obama was popular merely because he was black, not because he was qualified. Bill's statements backfired. Voters feared that, if Hillary won the election, there would be a two-headed president in the Oval Office: Billary. Obama's polls rose. Hers dropped.

Hillaryland staffers didn't know what to do to get her campaign back on track and their candidate back on top. For the first time, they quarreled. Her chief strategist, Mark Penn, argued that she should remain strong and not apologize for her vote on Iraq. Others retorted that she was coming across as a robot rather than a human being. Hillary considered firing campaign leaders, hiring new ones. She wasn't sure which way to turn.

Countdown

The 2008 presidential primary and caucus season opened at seven p.m. on January 3, in Iowa. A record number of nearly 240,000 voters gathered in local schools and churches to debate their options. Eight Democratic candidates appeared on the ballot. (Republicans had separate ballots.)

After an hour, they clustered in groups according to their preferences—Obama supporters in one area of a gym or cafeteria, Hillary supporters in another, et cetera. When the heads were counted, Obama had won. Hillary had not only lost: she had placed third, behind another candidate, Senator John Edwards.

Hillary was stunned. Only three months earlier, she had led in the polls. She rallied, however, and said, "What is most important now is that, as we go on with this contest . . . we answer the question . . . who will be the best president on Day One? I am ready for that contest."[364]

She firmly believed that she was "uniquely qualified" to be president. No one else had her level of experience or "firsthand knowledge of what goes on inside a White House."[365] She had seen close up that it's a tough job. Candidates who had not shouldn't try to cut in line.

Nevertheless, predictions indicated she would lose the next race too, five days later in New Hampshire. If she did, her run for the presidency might end as soon as the starting gun fired. She felt especially dejected when the moderator of a presidential debate there asked her why voters seemed to like Obama more than her.

"Well, that hurts my feelings," she responded.

Obama retorted, "You're likable enough, Hillary."[366]

On the morning before the New Hampshire primary, Hillary chatted with voters in a café in Portsmouth. One woman asked her, "How do you do it? . . . How do you keep upbeat?"[367]

"It's not easy," Hillary admitted. "I couldn't do it if I just didn't *passionately* believe it was the right thing to do." Her voice cracked as she added, "I just don't want to see us fall backwards. This is very personal for me. It's not just political . . . Some people think elections are a game—they think it's like who's up or who's down." Hillary shook her head. "It's about our country. It's about our kids' futures."

With tears in her eyes, she concluded, "As tired as I am—and I am . . . I just believe so strongly in who we are as a nation, so I'm going to do everything I can to make my case. Then the voters get to decide."[368] The group applauded.

The incident hit the news, and Hillary the Person appeared in people's living rooms that night. It turned out that she was not just a robot or a hawk. Voters caught a glimpse of a woman who sincerely cared about their families. Although they did not know the facts or details, here was a human being who had her father's guffaw, who called her friends on their birthdays and posted their children's drawings on her office wall.

As she told a reporter, "I'm probably the most famous person you don't really know."[369]

The next day, with polls projecting Obama the winner, so many people voted that officials feared they would run out of ballots. When the tally was counted that night, Hillary had won. She was the first woman to win delegates to a presidential convention in a primary election.

"Over the last week, I have listened to you," she told her supporters. "And in the process I found my own voice."[370] The race was still on.

JANUARY 19: Hillary won in Nevada.

JANUARY 26: Obama beat her in South Carolina.

JANUARY 29: Hillary took the lead in Florida. Edwards dropped out, as had the other candidates.

Two unlikely contenders remained—an African American and a woman. Both tried to avoid talking about the obvious issues. Nevertheless, charges of racism and sexism intruded into their campaigns. She found his comment about her likability and another he made about her clothes inappropriate. He found Bill's statement about his race tactless. Their hard feelings toward each other toughened.

Voters, many of whom were excited about the possibility of the country's first female or black president, seemed torn. Black women, especially, felt the dilemma.

Which candidate should they support?

Both were hopeful going into Super Tuesday on February 5. This was the date on which twenty-two states (plus American Samoa) would hold primaries and caucuses. It was also the date by which Hillary had assumed, a year earlier, that she would win enough delegates to clinch the nomination.

FEBRUARY 5: Hillary won nine states; Obama, thirteen. In terms of the number of delegates each acquired, the contest was a draw. In terms of expectations, Hillary lost. Her staff shouted at each other. The cash box was almost empty. She had to use $5 million of her own money to cover expenses. "We were running on fumes,"[371] one aide admitted. Everyone had been so sure that she would glide to victory, they didn't have a backup plan.

FEBRUARY 9–19: Obama won all of the next nine elections.

DELEGATE SCORE, FEBRUARY 19: Obama— 1,315. Clinton—1,245.

Wins and losses teeter-tottered back and forth through the spring as the candidates hopscotched around the country. They gave hundreds of speeches, shook thousands of hands, recorded dozens of ads, raised millions of dollars, flew tens of thousands of miles, staggering on and off airplanes late at night and early in the morning. The process was expensive and exhausting.

They jabbed at each other and wrestled for voters. She said she felt like a piñata. Older and low-income Americans as well as women tended to support her. Younger and better-educated people as well as African Americans leaned toward him. A few big states with lots of delegates joined her column. He gained a number of smaller ones.

In March, Hillary made a whopping mistake, by telling a whopper. In 1996, she and Chelsea had visited Bosnia, a region in Eastern Europe suffering from ongoing conflicts.

"I remember landing under sniper fire," Hillary told several groups. "We ran with our heads down."

But they didn't. They were greeted at the airport by schoolchildren. When reporters pointed out the facts, she responded, "I was sleep-deprived . . . I misspoke . . .

I don't know what I was thinking."[372] Americans questioned whether Hillary was telling the truth about the experiences that she claimed made her ready to be president. Her popularity sank.

Hillary fired and hired staff. Dorothy stood beside her on platforms. Chelsea dipped in and out of more than a hundred college campuses on behalf of her mother.

DELEGATE SCORE, MAY 13: Obama—1,884. Clinton—1,718.

Obama urged Hillary to concede. But "in to win" until the end, she "refused to quit until the last vote was counted."[373]

Why did she persist? Even after everyone, except perhaps Hillary herself, recognized that she couldn't reach the magic number of 2,118 delegates?

"This is one of the most important elections America has ever faced,"[374] she declared. It was critical to repair the damage she saw done by President Bush. The war had destroyed much of Iraq, along with America's reputation. And his policies threatened to destroy the economy at home.

As a staffer explained, "You still stay in it because you're committed to these people and this agenda that you've been championing . . . You can't give up on it because then you're letting people down."[375]

Hillary did—and does—not quit.

Down and Out of the Running

The end of Hillary's run for the Democratic presidential nomination came on June 3, 2008. Primaries that day in Montana and South Dakota, plus pledges from superdelegates, raised Obama's total to more than 2,200 delegates. With fewer than 1,900, Hillary could not possibly catch up. About eighteen million people had voted for her. But the math problem called for delegates.

"It was personally painful . . . a sense of real loss and disappointment," she admitted. "I did feel like I had let a lot of people down . . . a lot of women and girls who had invested their hopes in me."[376]

Like the coach of a defeated team, she congratulated Obama. He asked her to meet with him. Although she was angry and aching, she agreed to do so. Two days later, she lay down on the backseat of a minivan with tinted windows to slip past the reporters stationed in front of her house and was driven to a secret meeting.

They stared at each other, she said, "like two teenagers on an awkward first date."[377] He broke the ice by asking her a tough question. Would she and her team support him for the presidential election in November? Without unity, the Democrats could lose. After talking candidly about the ways each had felt insulted by the other during the primary battles, she agreed to work for him.

Beginning at dawn on June 7, throngs of disappointed Hillary fans lined up outside Washington's National Building Museum. This was the only space cavernous enough to hold her concession speech. Some people traveled from as far away as Pennsylvania to hear her in person. Many wondered if Obama would choose her as his vice presidential running mate.

Rousing cheers and applause greeted Hillary. Just six months earlier, she had been certain that she would be holding a victory celebration. Instead, she opened by saying, "Well, this isn't exactly the party I'd planned." Dorothy wiped away tears. Bill and Chelsea looked downcast.

Hillary went on to thank those who had worked for her. They included a thirteen-year-old girl in Ohio named Ann Riddle who used the money she had been saving for a trip to Disney World to volunteer in Pennsylvania instead. For young activists like Ann, Hillary advised, "Always aim high, work hard, and care deeply about what you believe in. When you stumble, keep faith. When you're knocked down, get right back up. And never listen to anyone who says you can't or shouldn't go on."

Hillary also acknowledged women like her mother, who were born before women could vote in America. Many had cast their ballots for Hillary. "From now on," she pointed out, "it will be unremarkable for a woman to win primary state victories . . . unremarkable to think that a woman can be the president of the United States. And that is truly remarkable."

She referred to the invisible barrier that has kept women from reaching the tip-top of their professions. "Although we weren't able to shatter that highest, hardest glass ceiling this time, thanks to you, it's got about eighteen million cracks in it." The throng roared. She continued, "And the light is shining through like never before, filling us all with the hope and the sure knowledge that the path will be a little easier next time." The next time, that is, a woman runs for president.

Finally, Hillary called on her cheering supporters to "do all we can to help elect Barack Obama the next president of the United States."[378] That's what she had promised the winner she would do.

Some of her followers had a hard time giving up their dream of seeing her on the ticket. So did she. But she soon made it clear that she was not interested in running for vice president.

· ·

PING-PONG!

When Hillary returned to her Senate office, she walked into an unexpected scene. Her staffers, dressed in gym shorts, headbands, and striped kneesocks, were playing Ping-Pong! To lighten the mood after her loss, they hauled in a table and played a game. "I love this!" Hillary guffawed. She advised the staffer who lost the match, "Be gracious in defeat."

· ·

Unity

Hillary kept her promise to the man at the top of the ticket in several ways. She immediately updated her website to read, "Support Senator Obama Today."[379]

At the end of June, the two former rivals appeared together in Unity, New Hampshire. They chose the town not only because of its name but also because each had received exactly 107 votes there in the primary.

"We stand shoulder to shoulder," she told the gathering, which chanted, "Thank you, Hillary. Thank you, Hillary."[380]

The audience that heard her message of unity two months later was massively larger. Five thousand delegates and politicians converged on Denver in August for the 2008 Democratic National Convention. Waving banners and wearing funny hats, they attended four days of speeches, rallies, debates, and, most important, the roll-call vote.

At the 1992 convention, Hillary knew that twelve-year-old Chelsea was too young to introduce her father. Now Chelsea was a poised twenty-eight-year-old.

Calling her mother "my hero,"[381] she introduced her via a video she had narrated. The hall greeted Hillary with a long and loud standing ovation.

"Whether you voted for me, or voted for Barack," she exclaimed when they finally quieted, "the time is now to unite as a single party with a single purpose. We are on the same team."[382]

On the convention's third night, the states are called in alphabetical order to cast their votes for the presidential nominee. By the time the chair recognized "the great state of New York," more than 340 delegates had indicated their preference for Hillary—the most ever for a female candidate. But Obama had racked up nearly 1,550 votes.

She strode into the convention center and proclaimed, "Let's declare together in one voice right here, right now, that Barack Obama is our candidate and he will be our president!"[383] With this statement, she called on the delegates to pronounce Obama their nominee by acclamation; that is, by unanimous voice vote. With cheers and roars, they did.

For the good of the country, Hillary abandoned her

quest for the presidency and helped her former opponent achieve his. This act may have been one of the hardest and bravest she'd ever taken.

What Went Wrong?

Not long after the convention, Hillary visited her college friend Jan Piercy. Jan's husband, Glenn, was dying. When she walked into their house, he struggled to rise from his chair.

"Oh, Glennie," the defeated candidate said, "don't stand up. It's not as if the president came to call."

"I'll never forget that," Jan later said. Hillary was "making light of herself after what had been a very, very painful loss."[384]

Hillary's election losses in 2008 were her first major failure since health-care reform died in 1994. The reasons differed. Again, she needed to think about where she went wrong:

Iraq

The war wasn't Hillary's fault. A total of twenty-eight other Democratic senators and forty-eight Republicans supported the resolution as well. But she had not studied the facts before she made her decision.

More important, she refused to apologize for her vote, even when the evidence showed there was no reason to invade Iraq. Even after soldiers returned home maimed or dead. Democrats did not want a president who would go to war at the hint of a threat, especially one that might be false.

"Saying you made a mistake," she knew, "is often taken as a weakness." Over time, she learned that apologizing "can be a sign of strength and growth." It took several years to admit that on Iraq, "I . . . got it wrong. Plain and simple."[385] She didn't state this clearly or soon enough, however, to win over primary voters.

Making Assumptions

In 2007, Hillary, her team, and much of the country assumed that the presidential nomination belonged to her. She was well-known, had accomplished a great deal, raised a lot of money, and had lived in the White House. A young, inexperienced senator did not seem to be a risk. Afterward she learned, "I don't take anything for granted. I have to earn your support."[386]

Strategy and Staff

Because she knew she would win, she didn't plan for the possibility that she might not. "I didn't have a good strategy for my campaign,"[387] she realized.

Her staff argued over where to advertise, how to get people to the polls, and what she should say. Sometimes she didn't state clearly what she believed; at other times, she said things that were not true. With Hillaryland in disarray, her control-from-the-top approach unraveled. Connecting with individuals through higher-tech methods than hers, Obama's grassroots strategy ruled.

Sexism

Comments by her opponents and the press about her appearance and her likability reminded Hillary that women are judged by different measures than men; however, she did not raise the issue. "I was not as effective calling it out during that campaign . . . because there is a double standard,"[388] she said.

As a woman, she believed she needed to appear strong. The electorate liked her, though, when she teared up. It was hard to figure out what Americans looked for in a female president. Could she be both tough and feminine?

"Like millions of women," Hillary said, "I know there are still barriers and biases out there, often unconscious."[389]

Yet again, Hillary turned to counting her blessings and practicing the discipline of gratitude. She was grateful that she could return to the US Senate to work for the citizens of New York.

"When Your President Asks You to Serve"

Between the convention and Election Day, Hillary and Bill appeared at about a hundred campaign events for Barack Obama. On November 4, 2008, he and his running mate, Senator Joe Biden, won. Soon, it would be the Obamas' turn to move into the White House. But first, the president-elect needed to fill his cabinet.

In mid-November, he asked Hillary to serve as his secretary of state. Even though rumors of the offer had spread through the press, she was "floored."[390] This was the most important position in the cabinet, fourth in line to the presidency, America's representative to the world.

Nevertheless, she told him that she wanted to keep her seat in the Senate. Also, she needed to earn money—more than the salary of a secretary of state—to pay off the loans she had made to her campaign. Obama rejected her rejection. He asked her to think about his request. She talked with Chelsea, Bill, friends, and staff, and turned him down again. He understood her concerns but asked her to keep thinking.

The two do-si-doed like square dancers for a week. Whenever she called him to decline the job, she was told he was in the bathroom and couldn't come to the phone!

"I want to get to yes," he insisted. "You're the best person for the job."[391]

Hillary stayed awake most of a night, pondering. Finally, she concluded, "When your president asks you to serve, you should say yes."[392]

In any case, John Wesley wouldn't let her say no. "Do all the good you can, by all the means you can, in all the ways you can, in all the places you can, at all the times you can, to all the people you can, as long as ever you can," he had advised. Around the world, there were billions of people whom, perhaps, she could help.

Hillary called the incoming president and accepted the position of secretary of state—another first for a former First Lady and, soon, a former senator.

Her appointment would not be official until she testified before the Senate Foreign Relations Committee and was confirmed by the full Senate. As usual, she did her homework. Her hearing lasted five hours, and she answered questions ranging from the Arctic to Tanzania. One conservative Republican praised "her impressive skills, her compassion, her collegiality."[393] The Senate confirmed her with a vote of ninety-four to two.

With Chelsea by her side, she told her colleagues that leaving them was "like leaving family."[394] She had bloomed in the Senate—both as a politician in her own right and as a team player. She would need to do the same in the State Department. Hillary placed her hand on her father's Bible, which Bill held, as the judge swore her into office. She held a second ceremony with Bill, Chelsea, and Dorothy, just as she had done when she was sworn in as a senator.

CHAPTER 12

Madam Secretary
2009–2013

· ·

The Building in Foggy Bottom

Quick! Think of every country in the world at the same time. Egypt. Chile. Nepal. Sierra Leone. Australia. Guatemala. Lebanon. The Philippines. Vatican City. Is your head swiveling? That's what life is like for America's secretary of state. Something is always happening somewhere, and everything is an emergency. When Hillary arrived at the US Department of State on January 22, 2009, it seemed as if the whole world was clamoring for her attention.

The headquarters for the staff that conducts America's relationships with other countries is located in a low-lying area of Washington, DC, about five blocks from the White House. Because the neighborhood was prone to sinking into fog and smog, it is called Foggy Bottom. With nearly five thousand rooms and eighty-four hallways, the eight-story structure is so sprawling and clunky it is known simply as "the Building."

On her first day as secretary of state, Hillary walked along the red carpet, laid out for her ceremonial entrance, into its soaring granite lobby. Across the way, colorful flags from more than two hundred countries fluttered along picture windows. Hundreds of employees surged around and above her on balconies and stairways, cheering, clapping, and calling, "We love you, Hillary!"[395] She grinned and waved back. Like her, many had worried that America's standing in the world had plummeted during George W. Bush's presidency. They sensed that the new president and his secretary of state would make things right.

Those who greeted her were a small fraction of her staff. About fifteen thousand people work in the US for the state department, most of them in the Building and other sites in DC. Another sixty-five thousand or so work at America's 270 embassies and other posts around the world. These include the United States Agency for International Development (USAID), which works to end poverty and promote good health abroad. In one day, Hillary leaped from managing a staff of thirty people in her Senate office to directing more than eighty thousand across the globe!

The stakes were suddenly higher, too. As one of a hundred senators, she could vote for or against an American war. As secretary of state, she would be responsible for trying to prevent international warfare. Worse, if she—or a translator—said something inappropriate, the US homeland could be at risk of attack.

Hillary had been thinking about the role of government in people's lives—that is, how much the government should help Americans in need—ever since she heard her parents arguing when she was a child. Her father claimed that people should stand on their own two feet. Her mother was more softhearted. As secretary of state, Hillary's perspective expanded. Now, she pondered what the American government should and should not do in foreign countries.

The outgoing secretary of state, Condoleezza Rice, had advised her to "pick a few big issues"[396] and focus on those. Some administrations, for instance, focused on bringing peace in the Middle East or fighting terrorism. But that wasn't Hillary's way. She was determined to "pay attention to the whole chessboard"[397]—that is, every place on the planet. So, she rode the private elevator directly to her cherrywood-paneled office on the seventh floor of the Building and started her new job.

In the Senate, Hillary had reached across the aisle to make friends with her opponents. At State, she reached across oceans to hold conversations with America's foes as well as its allies. She began by calling foreign leaders.

"Hi, this is Hillary," she said sociably. "How are you, Mr. Minister?"[398]

Most were pleased to chat with this world-famous powerhouse. The heads of China's Communist Party, however, responded, "Is the United States giving up on the Asian Pacific? We don't see you. You never come."[399]

Pivot to Asia: "Find Common Ground and . . . Stand Our Ground"

A secretary of state's first trip to a foreign country is even more important than a new senator's first speech.

Hillary predicted that Asia, especially the People's Republic of China, would become increasingly powerful in the twenty-first century. The most populous nation in the world, China had acted like a bully since the Communists took over in 1948. The Party controls the economy and the press, suppresses human rights, pollutes the environment, is expanding its military, and is seen as a threat to America and other democracies.

On the other hand, China is important for American businesses, which hire workers there to sew clothes and make telephones for us, among other products. And these companies would like to sell goods made at home to billions of Chinese citizens.

Hillary would need to be both candid and careful. She decided that the US should "pivot"[400] attention to that part of the world and figure out both "how to find common ground and how to stand our ground."[401] So, in February 2009, on her first excursion as secretary of state, she flew east to Japan, Indonesia, South Korea, and, finally, China.

HOW DID THE SECRETARY TRAVEL?

Blue-and-white Boeing 757 jets, called SAM (Special Air Missions), transported the secretary of state, her staff, and the press corps around the globe. Hillary had a personal compartment with a desk, sleeper couch, bathroom, map of the world, and private phone lines. She needed creature comforts because, over four years, she spent a total of 2,084 hours (almost eighty-seven days) on SAM.

Sometimes, flight attendants shopped for food along the route. Hillary especially enjoyed Oaxaca cheese in Mexico and tropical fruit in Cambodia. Because of time-zone shifts, though, passengers might be served beef stew when their stomachs said it was breakfast time. Once when her SAM broke down in a far-off place, she had to hitch a ride home with officials in the vicinity.

As secretary, Hillary spent 401 days on the road and traveled 956,733 miles (that's farther than thirty-eight times around the world at its circumference).

The department's Asia experts had prepared fat binders packed with the detailed information that she and her caravan of staff would need—the history, politics, laws, leaders, economy, geography, culture, languages, food, tourist sites, maps, weather forecasts, clothing, and manners in every place on their itinerary. Called the Book, this encyclopedia was stamped "CLASSIFIED" in red across the cover. Hillary took advantage of the long series of flights and refueling stops over the Pacific and across the Asian continent to study and absorb the Book's contents. Five days and three countries after leaving Washington, she landed in Beijing.

Hillary had returned to China only once since her dramatic appearance at the World Conference on Women in 1995. Women activists had been thrilled when she declared, "Women's rights are human rights."[402] Her Chinese hosts, however, had been livid. The official Party newspaper, *People's Daily*, published one line about her talk: "American Mrs. Clinton made a speech."[403] Now, in 2009, American Mrs. Clinton needed to be tactful yet firm, to show that America could cooperate but was still a superpower.

One of the leaders she met with was the top foreign

officer, State Councilor Dai Bingguo. On previous visits, the two had traded gifts. He brought one for Chelsea, and Hillary gave him one for his baby grand-daughter. Before getting down to work this time, they shared family photographs, finding common ground through their children. She agreed with Dai when he said, "This is what we're in it for."[404] Diplomacy, Hillary knew, involves not only debating issues but also relating to people. "You cannot ask people to make hard choices if they don't really know you and you haven't developed a level of trust and understanding,"[405] she said.

Hillary wanted this vast country to work with the US on improving the world economy. She made the point by quoting an ancient Chinese proverb. "When you are in a common boat, you need to cross the river peacefully together."[406] Her hosts were impressed, and the two opposing superpowers began to find a few ways to cooperate.

Still, Hillary stood her ground on human rights. Just as she had in 1995, she met with a group of women's rights activists. She urged them to keep working for equality between men and women and to proclaim, "I am not going to be quiet."[407] To support them and other such groups elsewhere, she created a new, temporary position in the State Department: ambassador for global women's issues, filled by her former White House chief of staff, Melanne Verveer.

This convening, as Hillary continued to call such gatherings, also promoted two beliefs that were important to her. First, women matter. Where women are not valued, the entire society suffers. And when societies suffer, the world is unsafe. Second, diplomacy isn't just for diplomats.

Smart Power in Shanghai

"Ni hen lihai!" a pair of American college students yelled through bullhorns in perfect Mandarin Chinese. "You are awesome!"

They were two of 160 student ambassadors who greeted visitors to the USA Pavilion at the Shanghai Expo in May 2010. The local Chinese were amazed that Americans could speak their language. Yet the US almost failed to show up at the expo because of the cost.

When Hillary had learned in 2009 that America did not plan to attend, she was embarrassed, and Dai was offended. She encouraged corporations to donate money because she believed that personal contact between citizens is an important way to improve relations between countries. The pavilion was constructed in record time, and during the next six months, seven million visitors marveled at American products and Chinese-speaking students.

Hillary called this form of unofficial diplomacy "smart power." In other examples, State Department personnel taught foreign NGOs how to use social media technology to spread democracy abroad. And American experts helped poor countries develop their economies. Smart power became Hillary's signature style as secretary of state.

· ·

SMART POWER

According to Hillary, smart power combines five strategies that the US can use to influence other countries.

1. Encourage allies to cooperate and become partners in improving the world.
2. Communicate and negotiate even with those who disagree with us.

3. Help other countries develop their economies, especially by educating women, sharing technology, and providing expertise.
4. Coordinate our policies to make sure they don't conflict with each other.
5. Maintain a strong economy in America and demonstrate ethical values.

. . . .

Dai was pleased with America's presence at the expo. Two months after it opened, however, he became furious with "American Mrs. Clinton" at a meeting in Vietnam. He made it clear that China planned to control the South China Sea, even though many countries along its shores needed access to it. When Hillary sided with the other countries, Dai exclaimed, "Why don't you 'pivot' out of here?"[408] In other words, scram! She did not. The sea issue was not resolved but Hillary showed the rest of Asia that America could stand up to a bully.

Back in the Office

On the way home from her foreign travels, Hillary could finally relax. She napped, leafed through magazines, chatted with Hillarylanders about their romances, and screened movies. On one flight, they watched a spy film in which a character announced, "Can't trust a woman in a pantsuit. Men wear the pants. The world doesn't need any more Hillary Clintons."[409] A planeload of aides and reporters burst out laughing. Hillary guffawed.

During the trip from Vietnam to DC, however, she had other matters on her mind—Chelsea's wedding, only a week away. Thirty-year-old Chelsea was marrying Marc Mezvinsky. The couple became friends in college but the families had known each other for years. Both of Marc's parents had served in Congress. And his mother had headed the American delegation to Beijing in 1995 when Hillary proclaimed that women's rights are human rights.

Unlike Hillary's informal ceremony, Chelsea and Marc's took place over a weekend, in August 2010, at an estate in New York's Hudson Valley. Calling herself "MOTB" for Mother of the Bride, Hillary had approved flowers and other arrangements from afar by email.

"I felt lucky," the MOTB said, "that my day job had

prepared me for the elaborate diplomacy required to help plan a big wedding."[410] She admitted that she had trouble paying attention to the president during a meeting in the Oval Office just days before the big event.

Ordinarily, however, the two leaders worked closely, and she met with him almost weekly. Hillary was especially pleased to see him on March 22, 2010—the day after the House of Representatives passed the Patient Protection and Affordable Care Act. Although this health-care reform act was weaker than the one she had developed, the country would finally get managed care. They grinned and hugged.

In addition to representing America around the world, Hillary ran the entire State Department. Whether at home or abroad, her schedule, a speechwriter said, "was intense and relentless."[411]

Most days began with her reading a pile of news clips that a staffer gathered around four in the morning. These kept Hillary up-to-date on the world in general. (He made sure to include stories about Bill and Chelsea's activities too.) In addition, she received a top-secret report on the status of terrorist threats. At 8:45 a.m., she met with her senior advisors.

Then she powered through back-to-back conferences, speeches, diplomatic events, phone calls, and quick decisions about foreign hot spots. If world affairs got especially stressful, she could turn to a gift from a previous secretary—a teddy bear that sang "Don't Worry, Be Happy" when she squeezed its paw.

Hillary left the Building in the evening carting a massive briefing book stuffed with materials for the next day. (This one included funny cat cartoons.) She studied her homework overnight.

Rushing to the White House one evening several months after she started the job, Hillary fell and broke her elbow. President Obama advised her to slow down. "It's a marathon, not a sprint,"[412] he said. After her elbow healed, she resumed full-speed ahead.

"I Couldn't Tell Anyone"

In March 2011, Hillary began slipping quietly out of the Building and popping up secretly at the White House. If even her closest aides asked where she'd gone, her scheduler said simply, "Meeting."[413]

What was so hush-hush? After a manhunt that had

lasted almost ten years, the Central Intelligence Agency believed it had finally located the world's most notorious terrorist—Osama bin Laden. He was hiding in a large house in a suburban town in Pakistan.

"I couldn't tell anyone,"[414] Hillary later said. If bin Laden knew he'd been found, he would escape again. He had already evaded American forces in Afghanistan.

Over the next six weeks, President Obama, Vice President Biden, Hillary, and a small number of other highest-level officials debated what to do. Some opposed taking any action. They worried that an operation would be too dangerous and would harm US relations with Pakistan. Others argued about the best strategy for an attack.

Hillary made the case for dropping Navy SEALs (Sea, Air, Land Teams) from helicopters onto bin Laden's house. She had studied the intelligence reports. She had also stood atop the Pile at Ground Zero in New York City and talked with first responders. For her, the matter was both tactical and personal.

"We should go for it,"[415] she urged. The president agreed.

The night before the raid, Hillary attended the wedding of one of Chelsea's friends. A guest asked her, "Secretary Clinton, do you think we'll ever get bin Laden?"

"I sure hope so,"[416] she simply said.

On May 1, 2011, she and the few others who knew what was about to take place gathered at the White House. They watched in real time as the SEALs landed. "I held my breath,"[417] Hillary said.

Despite a few mishaps, the mission succeeded. The SEALs killed bin Laden, as planned. After it was all over, President Obama called George W. Bush and then Bill.

"Hillary probably told you," the president began.

"I don't know what you're talking about,"[418] Bill responded. Hillary had kept the secret even from him.

When local college students heard the news, they congregated outside the gates of the White House, chanting, "USA! USA!" Exhausted from the tension and long hours, Hillary said, "I stood still and let the shouts and cheers wash over me."[419] Later, she called leaders in Pakistan to explain why the US military had landed in their country unannounced.

Only five months later, however, on November 1, 2011, Hillary felt as grief-stricken as she had felt euphoric on May 1. Her mother, Dorothy Howell Rodham, died at age ninety-two. One of Hillary's fondest memories was a statement her mother often made: "Life is not about what happens to you, but about what you do with what happens to you."[420] Both women made a lot happen.

"Better to Be Caught Trying"

The following year, Hillary found herself in another confrontation with Dai. The Communist Party had sentenced a blind man named Chen Guangcheng to house arrest because he demanded assistance for disabled people and criticized corrupt officials. In April 2012, Chen escaped. Although he had broken his foot jumping over a wall, he had made his way hundreds of miles to Beijing. As a human-rights activist, he pleaded for refuge in the American Embassy.

Chen's request shot up the chain of command to the secretary; however, it put her in a tight spot. On the one hand, she believed America should aid dissidents (people who disagree with their governments). On the other hand, she didn't want to infuriate Dai again. Because Chinese security officers were closing in on Chen, Hillary had less than an hour to decide whether or not to protect him. When Hillary and Bill were uncertain about whether or not to take a risk, they often advised each other, "Better to be caught trying."[421] Hillary ordered Embassy staff, "Go get him."[422] The country, she decided, had to act. America's values were at stake.

An embassy vehicle picked him up and sped to the American compound. But when he arrived, he demanded to be flown to the US. The Chinese government, however, refused to let him leave.

Republicans lambasted Hillary, charging that she couldn't handle a hobbled villager, let alone the Communist Party. The best hope for a solution was for Hillary to sit down with Dai one-on-one. Fortunately, she had developed a working relationship with him. She proposed a deal that both allowed Chen and his family to emigrate to the US and also saved face for China. Dai reluctantly agreed. Through personal diplomacy, Hillary converted a crisis into a triumph.

"She was especially good at assessing the personalities of foreign leaders and understanding how to connect to them," a Hillaryland staffer observed. "The way she studied and managed to deal with the Chinese leadership was really kind of breathtaking."[423]

Her chief of staff was so impressed with Hillary's abilities that she referred to her as "Secretary of Awesome."[424]

The basic issue involved not just Chen and China but also America's role in the world. How much should the US government do inside another nation? This question arose many times and places while Hillary served as secretary of state.

"The Whole World Comes at You Every Single Day"

China was only one of 112 countries Hillary visited as secretary of state, many of them more than once. She broke all previous secretaries' travel records. Sometimes, she dipped in and out of two or three in a single day. Why did she hop, skip, and jump around so much? As she learned in China, showing up in person matters.

"If you're not paying attention, people are going to feel like somehow they're not important to you,"[425] she said.

The flight-plan officer who arranged her routes pointed out, "It's a good thing the earth is round. Everything is always on the way to somewhere else."[426]

Her exhausted aides wondered how she overcame time zone changes and sixteen-hour flights to remain alert through lengthy negotiations. She even mustered energy to sightsee at temples in Cambodia and shop for rugs in India. As First Lady, she had carried jars of salsa and Tabasco sauce for jolts of energy. As secretary, she kept her eyelids open by drinking cup after cup of tea or coffee and digging her fingernails into her palm.

She had to keep going. There were so many problems to fix. A State Department officer explained, "The whole world comes at you every single day."[427] In Hillary's case, she also went *to* the world. For example:

Haiti, 2010

After an earthquake killed or injured more than half a million people in Haiti, the island's president said, "I need Hillary."[428] She canceled a trip to Asia and flew to the capital city to make sure medicines, tents, and other supplies were provided. Her aides helped orphans find new homes.

Burma, 2011

Hillary met Aung San Suu Kyi, a human-rights activist, who had recently been released from house arrest after fifteen years. The two women immediately became good friends. When Suu Kyi was elected to Parliament, the State Department helped her try to make Burma more fair.

Egypt, Tunisia, and Libya, 2011

During the period called the "Arab Spring," rebels rose up to replace dictators with democratic governments. Hillary persuaded European and Middle Eastern countries to support the rebels. The State Department supplied them with telecommunications. This was smart power in action. She even argued successfully for invading Libya, which toppled its cruel leader, Muammar Gaddafi.

"TEXTS FROM HILLARY"

A photograph of Hillary checking her cell phone went viral when Tumblr users paired it with photos of other people and concocted funny captions. One showed President Obama lying on a couch, messaging her, "Hey, Hil, watchu doing?" Her made-up response: "Running the world."[429] Chelsea referred to her mother as TechnoMom.

. . . .

Despite America's involvement, many issues were not solved, and countries remained unsettled. The US could not repair the whole world. In Libya, as in other Arab lands, the rebels overthrew the dictators but didn't know how to create a new government. They went at each other and even came after America.

"A Punch in the Gut"

Every September 11, Hillary recalled the horrifying day in 2001 when al Qaeda flew planes into the World Trade Center and the Pentagon. On the same date in

2012, Americans were attacked again. In midafternoon, Hillary learned that dozens of men had shot at and set fire to a State Department outpost in Benghazi, the second largest city in Libya. One American was dead. Others, including Ambassador Chris Stevens, were missing.

Hearing about the attack hit her like "a punch in the gut,"[430] she said. Stevens was a friend, and she had asked him to become ambassador to this troubled country. He spoke Arabic fluently, and knew many people there. She feared that she had put him and other personnel in mortal peril.

Several days earlier, thousands of young men in Egypt had staged demonstrations against an anti-Muslim movie made by an American citizen. Believing that the US had insulted their religion, they invaded the embassy in Cairo. Had protests in Egypt spread to Libya?

Hillary got to work trying to protect Americans by rounding up support from other agencies and staff in the capital city and everywhere else she could think of. She issued orders—and prayers. The president, the Central Intelligence Agency, and the military were also involved. But no one could tell what was happening in the danger zone. Over the telephone, they heard gunfire and grenades. Stevens still had not surfaced.

Later that evening, Hillary got word that he had died in the fire. Security personnel were also killed. She was heartbroken, as were the thousands at the State Department. Four of their own had fallen in service to their country.

Hillary somberly met the flag-draped caskets when they arrived on US soil, and grieved with family members. Emotional but resilient as always, she said, "We will wipe away our tears, stiffen our spines, and face the future undaunted."[431]

The presidential election was only two months away, and Obama was running again. Hoping to weaken his chance of winning, Republicans blamed Hillary for causing Stevens's death. Government investigations agreed that security was not strong enough in Benghazi but concluded that Hillary had reacted promptly and responsibly. She was angry that Republicans turned the tragedy into a political fight.

In defending herself, her explanation went to the heart of America's role in the world. "We need to be in dangerous places," she said. "I don't think we should be retreating from the world."[432]

"Beaches and Speeches"

After four years of nearly nonstop global travel, Hillary confessed, "I'm tired."[433] In just the five weeks between November 1 and December 7, 2012, she slipped in and out of thirteen countries. Then, she fell. She had picked up a stomach virus, become dehydrated, and fainted, hitting her head so hard that she suffered a concussion. She was out of work for a month.

When she finally returned to the office, her staff gave her a football helmet and a jersey with the number 112 on the back for the number of countries she'd visited. "As you know, Washington is a contact sport,"[434] a deputy said. She let loose with her typical laugh. But she was ready, she realized, to fill her time with nothing but "beaches and speeches."[435]

On February 1, 2013, Hillary returned to the department's lobby to greet her aides, this time in farewell. "I'm proud of the work we've done to elevate diplomacy and development, to serve the nation we all love,"[436] she told them.

People debate how much better off the world was after Hillary's four years as Madam Secretary. Some point out that there were no major peace treaties, and that wars continued in many trouble spots. Others say that smart power helped strengthen nongovernmental organizations and ordinary citizens—changes that will continue to do good for years.

President Obama showed his respect for her by making the position of ambassador for global women's issues a permanent one at the State Department. Hillary's efforts on behalf of women's equality around the world would carry on without her.

For the first time since leaving the Rose Law Firm over twenty years earlier, Hillary walked off without a job. But she had lots of plans in the works.

CHAPTER 13

The Next Ring
2013–2015

• •

Around the Kitchen Table

Before Hillary Rodham Clinton was secretary of state, senator from New York, First Lady of the United States, First Lady of Arkansas, a corporate lawyer, a law professor, a presidential campaign organizer, a law student, and a college student, she was a middle schooler who bought a First Communion dress for a seven-year-old girl named Maria in a migrant labor camp.

That experience touched Hillary and lived within her, inspiring her professional and volunteer activities on behalf of children, youth, and women for the next fifty years. In fact, it still does.

After leaving the State Department in February 2013, Hillary relaxed for the first time in years, spending time with family and friends, taking long walks with her dogs, catching up on movies, and sleeping late. Within six weeks, however, vacation was over, and she announced, "I've rested now. I'm ready to work."[437] She wrote a six-hundred-page book called *Hard Choices*, about the tough decisions she made as secretary of state. And she went on a nationwide book tour.

. . . .

HAIR HORROR—WHO CARES?

Hillary has said that she was tempted to title her latest book *The Scrunchie Chronicles: 112 Countries and It's Still All about My Hair.* Toward the end of her term as secretary, she gave up on stylists, let her hair grow long, and scrunched it into a ponytail, as she had in elementary school. No one accidentally tugged it off, as her friend Ricky had. But a journalist reported, "Clinton looks awful."[438]

By now, though, Hillary had learned an important lesson: "Don't let yourself get pulled down by other people's opinions because I think what you think about yourself, what you say to others about yourself really does affect how you present yourself and eventually who you are."[439] She was content with herself, floppy hairdo and all.

. . . .

Those activities might wear out most people—but not Hillary. While writing and giving talks, she also found new ways to devote herself to her lifelong commitments. These remained kitchen-table issues, but now the kitchens were all over the world.

Not long after leaving the White House, Bill established the Clinton Foundation to work on global health care, climate change, and other projects. When Hillary left the State Department, the organization grew, and it became the Bill, Hillary & Chelsea Clinton Foundation. Chelsea, who had worked as a business consultant, was named vice chairwoman of the board of directors. The three Clintons threw themselves into issues that concern them.

The foundation's motto is "We're all in this together"— a message similar to the title of Hillary's book *It Takes a Village*. It teams up with foreign governments, NGOs, nonprofit companies, corporations, and individuals to resolve global problems. Thinking about the role of government over her decades as a public servant, Hillary knew that government is essential for providing many services, including education, health care, and military defense. But some services work best, she realized, when government collaborates with partners.

"While Talent Is Universal, Opportunity Is Not"

Hillary focused on three favorite projects, which she worked on with the foundation and its cooperating groups. Her goal was to help people reach their full potential because, she says, "While talent is universal, opportunity is not."[440] Everybody is good at something, but they might need a boost to develop it.

Too Small to Fail

As First Lady, Hillary held a conference at the White House on how babies' brains grow. Experts pointed out that it's important for adults to talk, read, and sing to infants. But poor families tend to have less time for these activities than wealthy ones do, and they own fewer books. By the time children are four years old, research showed, wealthier kids have heard as many as thirty million more words. Their vocabularies are larger, and they tend to do better in school.

Ann O'Leary, who had been Hillary's deputy chief of staff at the Senate, formed a partnership with the Clinton Foundation and other groups to "close the word gap."[441] Through their program, Too Small to Fail, coaches go to nursery schools and homes to show parents and teachers how to talk, read, and sing with children. The project has even introduced these skills into television shows and movies. Hillary had a great time singing "Take Me Out to the Ball Game" with toddlers in Tulsa, Oklahoma. Maybe they didn't notice she couldn't carry a tune!

Hillary is also proud that the foundation is partnering with Reach Out and Read and with pediatricians. The doctors explain to parents how important it is to read, talk, and sing to their babies. Then the doctors hand out books to their young patients.

Job One

Hillary was also concerned about the six million Americans between the ages of eighteen and twenty-four who don't have jobs and aren't in school. How can they support themselves? she wondered.

"For those who haven't graduated from college or even high school, most doors just won't open, no matter how hard they knock,"[442] she said. At the same time, though, business leaders complain that they can't find skilled workers.

So, Hillary started Job One, a program that brings together corporations to set up training and mentoring for these youth. A wide variety of companies help them prepare for technical, financial, retail, manufacturing, hospitality, and other jobs.

No Ceilings: The Full Participation Project

After the United Nations World Conference on Women in 1995, the UN's Platform for Action set goals, including full participation by women in all aspects of society. A total of 189 countries agreed to try to meet the goals. But no one knew how close they were to achieving them—or how far they had to go.

Hillary wanted to know: How many girls finish elementary school? High school? How many women have the jobs they want and deserve? Are they paid the same as men? Do they win political races? Have these situations changed over time?

After twenty years, in 2015, she noted that more girls were finishing primary school but too many were not continuing their education. Also, not enough women were reaching the top in politics or business. Hillary believed that more efforts and information were needed.

To collect data about women's advances and the obstacles they face, Hillary and Chelsea started No Ceilings: The Full Participation Project. The name showed that they would not be satisfied even with eighteen million cracks in the ceiling. No Ceilings wants no limit to women's achievement.

"We're going to be about the business of making sure that those ceilings crack for every girl and for every woman around the globe," Hillary announced. "So let's get cracking!"[443]

. . . .

CHELSEA'S "BABIES"

In addition to working with her mother on No Ceilings, Chelsea has also created other projects. She encourages young people to volunteer in their communities by hosting Days of Action. At these events, she and sometimes hundreds of students work at food pantries, beautify parks and playgrounds, and clean up from hurricanes. With a PhD in global health, Chelsea also travels the world promoting awareness of malaria, testing for HIV, and ways to purify drinking water.

And, on September 26, 2014, she gave birth to Charlotte Clinton Mezvinsky. Holding her granddaughter for the first time, @HillaryClinton tweeted, "@BillClinton and I are over the moon to be grandparents! One of the happiest moments of our life."[444] Charlotte's nursery is decorated with elephants because one of Chelsea's projects is protecting elephants from poachers.

"When Bill and I get down on our hands and knees to play on the floor with Charlotte," Hillary said, "I find myself thinking back to . . . when my own father did the same with Chelsea. . . . I know exactly how he felt."[445] The new grandmother advised her daughter, "Pick what you liked about how we raised you, and do it. And if you'd rather make some changes, that's fine, too."[446]

The Clintons partnered with other groups to gather and share information ranging from high school education to salaries to political elections. A video describing the project explains, "We are counting women and girls because women and girls count."[447]

In addition to collecting data on women's progress, No Ceilings took action. A teenager who participated in a convening at New York's Lower Eastside Girls Club said that she learned "you don't have to be the way society wants you to be. You can be your own person."[448] Chelsea discovered that fewer women than men own cellular telephones. So, she looked into the gender gap in mobile technology. A third No Ceilings program brought together thirty partner organizations to reduce the gender gap in education for fourteen million girls. That could break through a lot of ceilings!

President Hillary?

In June 2013, Hillary opened a Twitter account. She described herself in her profile as "wife, mom, lawyer, women & kids advocate, FLOAR, FLOTUS, US

Senator, SecState, author, dog owner, hair icon, pant-suit aficionado, glass ceiling cracker, TBD . . ."[449] As a college student, she searched for an identity. Over the years, she created a unique one that is broad, impressive—and amusing. Within five days, Hillary's Twitter feed attracted nearly half a million followers.

• •

FOUR WORDS

A student asked Hillary, in 2014, to describe herself in three words. She did—and then added a fourth. Here they are:

- "Intense"
- "Passionate"
- "Service-minded"
- "Grateful"[450]

• •

But what did "TBD," which stands for "to be determined," mean? Was Hillary planning to run for president again? A lot of people were curious. The next election would be in 2016.

Supporters started forming political action committees (PACs) to raise money and encourage her to run. One of the biggest was called Ready for Hillary. She's the most qualified candidate, they asserted. She cares about low- and middle-income families. She understands world affairs and knows foreign leaders. She understands the pressures that a president faces and can make hard decisions. She's a loyal friend. Anyway, there's no one else, is there?

Opponents, however, also formed PACs, such as Stop Hillary. She's too old, some argued. She failed to protect Americans in Benghazi—how could she defend the homeland? She's a hawk, too eager to go to war. After leaving the State Department, she erased her emails, which she had kept on a private server, saving only the ones *she* decided were official. Can she be trusted? She and Bill asked foreign governments to pay for some of the foundation's projects. Is that a conflict of interest? Not another Clinton—anyone but her!

Hillary continued to be revered by some and reviled by others. She offended both followers and foes by claiming that she and Bill "came out of the White House not only dead broke but in debt."[451] Many people criticized her for charging $200,000 or more to give a speech. Voters wondered if she lived in a bubble, out of touch with ordinary citizens.

BRINGING AMERICANS TOGETHER AGAIN

Americans hold deep-seated—and often conflicting—opinions. As a result, Hillary worries that "we're appearing too often like we can't ever get together and solve our problems."[452] Two groups, she says, can unravel this dilemma. They are elected officials and the public, especially young people.

She urges office holders to work harder at building relationships, just as she did as senator and secretary of state. Furthermore, Hillary tells youngsters, "my advice is, always become . . . involved in politics."[453]

Through 2013 and 2014, they wondered whether she would run for president again. In speeches around the country, she hinted that she might by explaining her views about what makes a good leader.

Running for president isn't just a team sport. And it isn't just a math problem. The essential issues, she said, are a picture of the ideal America and the ability to achieve it. "What is your vision for our country? . . . Can you—with the tenacity, the persistence, the getting-knocked-down/getting-back-up resilience—lead us there?"[454]

In an updated ending to *Hard Choices*, she shared her vision of America—by referring to Charlotte. "You shouldn't have to be the granddaughter of a president or a secretary of state," Hillary wrote, "to receive excellent health care, education, enrichment, and all the support and advantages that will one day lead to a good job and a successful life."[455]

Finally, on April 12, 2015, Hillary declared her intention to lead the country in achieving that vision. She announced her second run for the presidential nomination by posting an online video, just as she had in 2007.

"I'm getting ready . . . to run for president," she stated, standing in front of her house in Chappaqua. "Everyday Americans need a champion. I want to be that champion." Her video featured a variety of families "because when families are strong, America is strong."[456]

Then, as she had ever since running for head of college government at Wellesley, she embarked on a listening tour. Hillary rode in a van, which she named Scooby, to Iowa, where she chatted with everyday Americans.

Some questioned whether a grandmother had the stamina to conduct another grueling campaign. Multiple Republican rivals announced their intentions to run against her. So did several Democrats. However, Hillary is proud of her "getting-knocked-down/getting-back-up resilience." She lost the fight for health care in 1994 and the presidential nomination in 2008. In between, she almost decided to lose Bill in 1998. Nevertheless, she got back up and kept going.

To do so, she's needed to learn from her mistakes. Looking back at them, she's had to think about:

- Strategies and goals: What are the right goals and the best ways to meet them?
- Compromise: How does a politician compromise on tactics while holding on to her values?
- Image and the media: How can a person who is always in the public eye be herself and let her hair down?

Every candidate faces these issues. For Hillary—or any other woman—there is an additional one:

- Sexism: How can she help make America ready for a female president?

Answering these questions correctly will help determine whether she grabs the next ring.

Making the Impossible Possible

In her graduation talk at Wellesley, Hillary stated, "for too long our leaders have viewed politics as the art of the possible." She added, "the challenge now is to practice politics as the art of making what appears to be impossible, possible."[457] Since then, she has become an international leader, one of the most powerful women in the world, and the most admired woman in America.

Perhaps Hillary Rodham Clinton will be the politician who will make America strong through strong families—and achieve what has so far been impossible: a woman whose West Wing office is the Oval Office.

TIMELINE

1947

Hillary Diane Rodham is born to Dorothy and Hugh Rodham in Chicago, Illinois, on October 26, 1947.

1950–1965

Hillary moves with her family to Park Ridge and attends Eugene Field Elementary School, Maine East High School, and Maine South High School, from which she graduates.

1965–1969

Hillary attends and graduates from Wellesley College, where she becomes a Democrat, is elected president of the College Government Association, and is the first student to give a commencement speech.

1969–1973

Hillary attends and graduates from Yale Law School, where she studies law and child development and works for Marian Wright Edelman. She meets Bill Clinton; they campaign in Texas for George McGovern, the Democratic presidential nominee.

1974
. . . .

Hillary works in Washington, DC, for the committee investigating the possible impeachment of President Richard M. Nixon.

1974–1976
. . . .

Hillary moves to Fayetteville, Arkansas, to be with Bill and teach law at the University of Arkansas. They marry on October 11, 1975.

1977–1979
. . . .

Hillary and Bill move to Little Rock when Bill is elected attorney general of Arkansas. Hillary joins the Rose Law Firm.

1979–1992
. . . .

Hillary serves as First Lady of Arkansas when Bill is elected governor in 1978, and she continues to practice law. She changes her name to Hillary Rodham Clinton after Bill loses reelection in 1980. Their daughter, Chelsea Victoria, is born on February 27, 1980. Hillary oversees statewide educational reform after Bill is reelected in 1982. She invests in the Whitewater Development Corporation and other ventures.

1992–1994

Following a grueling campaign in which Hillary is criticized, Bill is elected president of the United States. Hillary serves as First Lady of the United States and tries but fails to reform health care. In 1993, her father, Hugh Rodham, dies, and her friend Vince Foster from the Rose Law Firm commits suicide. She sees evidence of a right-wing conspiracy in attacks on her and Bill.

1994–1998

Special Prosecutor Ken Starr investigates her financial dealings. A grand jury finds her not guilty.

1995–2000

· ·

Hillary travels around the world promoting the importance of women and girls. She gives a speech in Beijing in 1995, saying, "Human rights are women's rights." She works to implement a Platform for Action in the US, and writes a newspaper column and three books—*Dear Socks, Dear Buddy: Kids' Letters to the First Pets*; *It Takes a Village: And Other Lessons Children Teach Us*; and *An Invitation to the White House*. Hillary also carries out the responsibilities of the First Lady—entertaining foreign heads of state, friends, and the public, and overseeing redecoration of the White House. Chelsea enrolls at Stanford University in 1997.

1998–1999

· ·

Hillary considers whether to stay married to Bill after he is accused of and finally admits to an inappropriate relationship with a female White House intern. Bill is impeached and is found not guilty.

2000–2008

Hillary and Bill move to New York and Hillary is elected to the US Senate, where she works with both Republicans and Democrats. After al Qaeda attacks the United States on September 11, 2001, she votes for President Bush's request to invade Iraq. She also writes another book, *Living History*.

2008

Hillary runs for nomination as a candidate for president of the United States. She receives about eighteen million votes but loses to Senator Barack Obama and then works for his election.

2009–2013

Hillary is appointed secretary of state by President Obama and visits 112 countries. She promotes policies such as "pivot to Asia," smart power, and the importance of women and girls. Chelsea gets married in 2010. Dorothy Rodham dies in 2011.

• •

Hillary writes *Hard Choices*, works on projects with the Bill, Hillary & Chelsea Clinton Foundation, and gives speeches. She becomes a grandmother in 2014. In April 2015, Hillary announces her second campaign for president of the United States.

AUTHOR'S NOTE

When people learn that I lived across the hall from Hillary Rodham during her freshman year of college, they ask if I remember her. "Of course!" I say. "She was a standout." And she was. At age seventeen, she stood out as a vibrantly curious and concerned young woman. It was my loss that I failed to keep up with her, except intermittently, over the years since then. Candidly, I was intimidated. However, while writing this book, it has been my pleasure and honor to get to know her again through other writers, through new and mutual acquaintances, and through her personal responses to several questions I posed. I hope I have learned to be less afraid.

ACKNOWLEDGMENTS

A book for young readers about Hillary Rodham Clinton can easily be filled simply with her many extraordinary ambitions and achievements. For this book, I set the additional goal of bringing this woman, who understandably covets her privacy, to life as a warm, funny, thoughtful, and humanly flawed person of faith. To the extent that I have succeeded, I am very grateful to the following people for sharing their stories and insights: Paul Begala, Janice Beinart, Philip Chase Bobbitt, Josh Daniel, Peter Edelman, Betty Sue Flowers, Jinnet Fowles, Bill Galston, Nancy Gist, Laura Grim, Laura Grosch, Susanne Jalbert, Nancy Kleeman, Garry Mauro, Nick Merrill, Lissa Muscatine, Alyse Nelson, Steve Nickles, Ann O'Leary, Kris Olson, Maura Pally, Jan Piercy, Lissa Piercy, Carol Hampton Rasco, Ann Rosewater, Joy Secuban, Dana S. Semeraro, Susan Sherwin, Gerald Torres, Melanne Verveer, Nancy Wanderer, Amity Weiss, and Heather Bastow Weiss. I was especially gratified that, without reading the manuscript before its publication, the secretary took the time during her presidential campaign to respond to questions.

In addition, I owe thanks to Kristin Daly Rens for handing me the next ring on the crossbars and to Erin Murphy for helping me grab it. As always, I deeply thank my thoroughly splendid family—Eli, Sarah, Ariel, Rachel, Ella, Rebecca, Meira, Marc, and above all, Sandy—for tolerating my disappearance as I immersed myself in All Things Hillary.

NOTES

1. Gail Sheehy, *Hillary's Choice* (New York: Random House, 1999), 26.
2. Ibid, 24.
3. Ibid, 25.
4. Ibid, 19.
5. Hillary Rodham Clinton, *It Takes a Village: And Other Lessons Children Teach Us* (New York: Simon & Schuster, 2006), 159.
6. Sheehy, *Hillary's Choice,* 43.
7. Hillary Rodham Clinton, email message to the author, May 11, 2015.
8. Hillary Rodham Clinton, *Living History* (New York: Simon & Schuster, 2003), 13–14.
9. Sally Jenkins, "Growing Up Rodham," *Washington Post*, December 9, 2007, http://www.washingtonpost.com/wp-dyn/content/story/2007/12/08/ST2007120801758.html.
10. Clinton, *It Takes a Village*, 15.
11. Ibid, 22.
12. Jenkins, "Growing Up Rodham."
13. Clinton, *Living History*, 48.
14. Bernstein, *A Woman in Charge*, 15.
15. Ibid, 25.

16. Clinton, *It Takes a Village*, 144.

17. Clinton, *Living History*, 12.

18. Clinton, *It Takes a Village*, 144.

19. Bernstein, *A Woman in Charge*, 25–26. (Italics in the original.)

20. Clinton, *It Takes a Village*, 136.

21. "MacArthur's Speeches: 'Old Soldiers Never Die . . . ,'" online transcript of General MacArthur's address to Congress, April 19, 1951, http://www.pbs.org/wgbh/amex/macarthur/filmmore/reference/primary/macspeech05.html.

22. Bob Dylan, "A Hard Rain's A-Gonna Fall," http://www.bobdylan.com/us/songs/hard-rains-gonna-fall.

23. Donnie Radcliffe, *Hillary Rodham Clinton: The Evolution of a First Lady* (New York: Grand Central Publishing, 1999), 45.

24. Clinton, *Living History*, 22.

25. Sheehy, *Hillary's Choice*, 36.

26. Hillary Rodham Clinton, email message to the author, May 11, 2015.

27. Sheehy, *Hillary's Choice*, 34.

28. Clinton, *Living History*, 12.

29. Ibid, 24.

30. Radcliffe, *Hillary Rodham Clinton*, 24.

31. Clinton, *Living History*, 24.

32. Radcliffe, *Hillary Rodham Clinton*, 24.

33. Bernstein, *A Woman in Charge*, 33.

34. Clinton, *Living History*, 17.

35. Jinnet Fowles, telephone interview with the author, July 8, 2014.

36. Miriam Horn, *Rebels in White Gloves: Coming of Age with Hillary's Class—Wellesley '69* (New York: Crown Publishing Group, 1999), 8.

37. Clinton, *Living History*, 27.

38. Ibid.

39. Sheehy, *Hillary's Choice*, 39.

40. Bernstein, *A Woman in Charge*, 103.

41. Kris Olson, telephone interview with the author, July 21, 2014.

42. Sheehy, *Hillary's Choice*, 39.

43. Radcliffe, *Hillary Rodham Clinton*, 61.

44. Mark Liebovich, "In Turmoil of '68, Clinton Found a New Voice," *New York Times*, September 5, 2007. http://www.nytimes.com/2007/09/05/us/politics/05clinton.html.

45. Horn, *Rebels in White Gloves*, 38.

46. Radcliffe, *Hillary Rodham Clinton*, 59.

47. Horn, *Rebels in White Gloves*, 35.

48. Nancy Wanderer, telephone interview with the author, July 12, 2014.

49. Horn, *Rebels in White Gloves*, 12.

50. Clinton, *Living History*, 32.

51. Dr. Martin Luther King, Jr., speech delivered at Riverside

Church, New York, New York, April 4, 1967.

52. Clinton, *Living History*, 31–32.

53. Olson interview.

54. Bernstein, *A Woman in Charge*, 50.

55. Ibid, 51.

56. *Legenda 1967*, Wellesley College yearbook, 14.

57. Bernstein, *A Woman in Charge*, 44.

58. Nancy Kleeman, telephone interview with the author, July 7, 2014.

59. Leibovich, "In Turmoil of '68, Clinton Found a New Voice."

60. Sheehy, *Hillary's Choice*, 51.

61. Bernstein, *A Woman in Charge*, 51.

62. Ibid, 53.

63. Clinton, *Living History*, 33.

64. Sheehy, *Hillary's Choice*, 45.

65. Clinton, *Living History*, 34.

66. Ibid, 36.

67. Ibid, 37.

68. Ibid.

69. Liebovich, "In Turmoil of '68, Clinton Found a New Voice."

70. Jeff Gerth and Don Van Natta Jr., *Her Way: The Hopes and Ambitions of Hillary Rodham Clinton* (New York: Little, Brown and Company, 2007), 38.

71. Clinton, *Living History*, 37.

72. Ibid, 38.

73. Ibid, 57.

74. Ibid, 39.

75. Edward Brooke, "Progress in the Uptight Society: Real Problems and Wrong Procedures," Commencement Address to the Wellesley College Class of 1969, May 31, 1969, http://www.wellesley.edu/events/commencement/archives/1969commencement/commencementaddress.

76. Hillary D. Rodham, Student Commencement Speech to the Wellesley College Class of 1969, May 31, 1969, http://www.wellesley.edu/events/commencement/archives/1969commencement/studentspeech.

77. Ibid.

78. Ibid.

79. Ibid.

80. Clinton, *Living History*, 41.

81. Horn, *Rebels in White Gloves*, 47.

82. Ibid, 46.

83. Clinton, *Living History*, 42.

84. Horn, *Rebels in White Gloves*, 47.

85. Clinton, *Living History*, 27.

86. Ibid, 44.

87. Nancy Gist, telephone interview with the author, July 16, 2014.

88. Liebovich, "In Turmoil of '68, Clinton Found a New Voice."

89. Clinton, *Living History*, 46.

90. Radcliffe, *Hillary Rodham Clinton*, 91.

91. Olson interview.

92. Clinton, *Living History*, 44.

93.   Radcliffe, *Hillary Rodham Clinton*, 95.

94.   Joyce Milton, *The First Partner: Hillary Rodham Clinton* (New York: William Morrow and Company, 1999), 44.

95.   Radcliffe, *Hillary Rodham Clinton*, 96.

96.   Clinton, *Living History*, 50.

97.   Olson interview.

98.   Clinton, *Living History*, 52.

99.   Ibid.

100. Bill Clinton, *My Life* (New York: Knopf, 2004), 182.

101. Radcliffe, *Hillary Rodham Clinton*, 104.

102. Olson interview.

103. Gist interview.

104. Clinton, *Living History*, 57.

105. Friend, telephone interview with the author, June 3, 2014.

106. Clinton, *Living History*, 58.

107. Ibid, 47.

108. Ibid, 58.

109. Garry Mauro, telephone interview with the author, July 14, 2014.

110. Bernstein, *A Woman in Charge*, 87.

111. Mauro interview.

112. Clinton, *Living History*, 60.

113. Ibid, 61.

114. Radcliffe, *Hillary Rodham Clinton*, 118.

115. Connie Bruck, "Hillary the Pol," *The New Yorker*, May 30, 1994.

116. Clinton, *Living History*, 63.

117. Radcliffe, *Hillary Rodham Clinton*, 118.
118. Children's Defense Fund of the Washington Research Project, Inc., *Children Out of School in America* (October 1974), 11, http://diglib.lib.utk.edu/cdf/data/0116_00005 0_000207/0116_000050_000207.pdf.
119. Clinton, *Living History*, 64.
120. Carroll Kilpatrick, "Nixon Tells Editors, 'I'm Not a Crook,'" *Washington Post*, November 18, 1973, http://www .washingtonpost.com/politics/nixon-tells-editors-im-not-a -crook/2012/06/04/gJQA1RK6IV_story.html.
121. Russell L. Riley, interview with Bernard Nussbaum. Miller Center of Public Affairs, University of Virginia, 2002, http://millercenter.org/president/clinton/oralhistory/ bernard-nussbaum-2002.
122. Bernstein, *A Woman in Charge*, 99.
123. Ibid, 90.
124. Clinton, *Living History*, 68.
125. Radcliffe, *Hillary Rodham Clinton*, 130.
126. Clinton, *Living History*, 69.
127. Radcliffe, *Hillary Rodham Clinton*, 127–28.
128. Gil Troy, *Hillary Rodham Clinton: Polarizing First Lady* (Lawrence, Kansas: University of Kansas Press, 2006), 24.
129. Clinton, *Living History*, 69.
130. Radcliffe, *Hillary Rodham Clinton*, 137.
131. Clinton, *Living History*, 69.
132. Radcliffe, *Hillary Rodham Clinton*, 137.
133. Jonathan Allen and Amie Parnes, *HRC: State Secrets and the Rebirth of Hillary Clinton* (New York: Crown

Publishing Group, 2014), 99.

134. Steve Nickles, telephone interview with the author, June 4, 2014.

135. Bernstein, *A Woman in Charge*, 109.

136. Clinton, *Living History*, 71.

137. Ibid, 70.

138. Ibid.

139. Ibid, 71.

140. Nickles interview.

141. Bernstein, *A Woman in Charge*, 114.

142. Ibid, 116.

143. Clinton, *Living History*, 74.

144. Bernstein, *A Woman in Charge*, 121.

145. Clinton, *Living History*, 75.

146. Nickles interview.

147. Radcliffe, *Hillary Rodham Clinton*, 170.

148. Ibid.

149. Clinton, *Living History*, 91–92.

150. Ibid, 82.

151. Ibid, 85.

152. Hillary Rodham Clinton, email message to the author, May 11, 2015.

153. Ibid.

154. Clinton, *Living History*, 85.

155. Bernstein, *A Woman in Charge*, 157.

156. Nickles interview.

157. Clinton, *Living History*, 91.

158. Lynn Vincent, "Reinventing Hillary," *World* magazine,

November 17, 2007, http://www.worldmag.com/2007/11/
reinventing_hillary/page1.

159. Clinton, *Living History*, 91.

160. Olson interview.

161. Clinton, *Living History*, 92.

162. Bernstein, *A Woman in Charge*, 165.

163. Clinton, *Living History*, 166.

164. Radcliffe, *Hillary Rodham Clinton*, 202–203.

165. "Standards for Accreditation of Arkansas Public
Schools," *Preliminary Report of the Education Standards
Committee* (September 1983), 5.

166. Clinton, *Living History*, 95.

167. Ibid, 94.

168. "Obama, Clinton, McCain and Frist Appeal to Parents
to #CloseTheWordGap," June 25, 2014, http://toosmall
.org/news/commentaries/obama-clinton-mccain-and
-frist-appeal-to-parents-to-closethewordgap.

169. Fowles interview.

170. Radcliffe, *Hillary Rodham Clinton*, 222.

171. Ibid.

172. Clinton, *Living History*, 107.

173. Ibid.

174. Ibid, 109.

175. Ibid.

176. Ibid, 105.

177. Mauro interview.

178. Clinton, *Living History*, 102.

179. Ibid, 103.

180. Fowles interview.

181. Radcliffe, *Hillary Rodham Clinton*, 195.

182. Paul Begala, telephone interview with the author, August 6, 2014.

183. Melanne Verveer, telephone interview with the author, August 30, 2014.

184. Clinton, *Living History*, 114.

185. Radcliffe, *Hillary Rodham Clinton*, 17–18.

186. Mauro interview.

187. Clinton, *Living History*, 117.

188. Nickles interview.

189. Clinton, *Living History*, 124.

190. Ibid, 125.

191. Sally Bedell Smith, *For Love of Politics: Inside the Clinton White House* (New York: Random House, 2008), 50.

192. Clinton, *Living History*, 136.

193. Ibid.

194. Hillary Rodham Clinton, email message to the author, May 11, 2015.

195. Hillary Clinton, "Talking It Over," July 23, 1995, www.creators.com/opinion/hillary-clinton.html.

196. Hillary Rodham Clinton, email message to the author, May 11, 2015.

197. Ibid.

198. Clinton, *Living History*, 119.

199. Elizabeth Kolbert, "The Student," *The New Yorker*, October 13, 2003.

200. "Eleanor Roosevelt," *American Experience*, season 12,

episode 6, directed by Sue Williams, aired January 10, 2000, http://www.pbs.org/wgbh/americanexperience/features/introduction/eleanor-introduction.

201. Begala interview.

202. Kati Marton, *Hidden Power: Presidential Marriages That Shaped Our Recent History* (New York and Canada: Anchor Books, 2002), 322.

203. William Galston, telephone interview with the author, August 20, 2014.

204. Melanne Verveer, email message to the author, January 28, 2015.

205. Clinton, *Living History*, 184.

206. Bernstein, *A Woman in Charge*, 330.

207. Smith, *For Love of Politics*, 91.

208. Troy, *Hillary Rodham Clinton*, 121.

209. Haynes Johnson and David S. Broder, *The System: The American Way of Politics at the Breaking Point* (New York: Little, Brown and Company, 1996), 136

210. Bernstein, *A Woman in Charge*, 297.

211. Smith, *For Love of Politics*, 107.

212. Clinton, *Living History*, 174.

213. R. W. Apple Jr., "Note Left by White House Aide: Accusation, Anger and Despair," *New York Times*, August 11, 1993.

214. Clinton, *Living History*, 178.

215. Smith, *For Love of Politics*, 126.

216. Clinton, *Living History*, 189.

217. Bernstein, *A Woman in Charge*, 396.

218. Johnson and Broder, *The System*, 184.

219. Bernstein, *A Woman in Charge*, 396.

220. "Harry and Louise on Clinton's Health Plan," YouTube video, 1:00, posted by "danieljbmitchell," July 15, 2007, https://www.youtube.com/watch?v=Dt31nhleeCg.

221. Carol Rasco, telephone interview with the author, September 4, 2014.

222. Smith, *For Love of Politics*, 146.

223. Clinton, *Living History*, 192.

224. Ibid.

225. Smith, *For Love of Politics*, 129.

226. Bernstein, *A Woman in Charge*, 356.

227. Michael Kelly, "Saint Hillary," *New York Times Magazine*, May 23, 1993.

228. Gist interview.

229. Smith, *For Love of Politics*, 157.

230. Johnson and Broder, *The System*, 473.

231. Clinton, *Living History*, 246.

232. Gerth and Van Natta Jr., *Her Way*, 140.

233. Clinton, *Living History*, 247.

234. Bernstein, *A Woman in Charge*, 371.

235. Clinton, *Living History*, 248.

236. Ibid, 171.

237. Ibid, 248.

238. Ibid.

239. Smith, *For Love of Politics*, 31.

240. Steve Nickles, telephone interview with the author, June 14, 2014.

241. Bernstein, *A Woman in Charge*, 410.

242. R. W. Apple Jr., "The 1994 Elections," *New York Times*, November 10, 1994.

243. "Election Results Show Voters Are Fed Up." *San Jose Mercury News*, November 10, 1994.

244. "Democrats Go Down in a Riptide of Voters' Discontent." *Minneapolis Star Tribune*, November 10, 1994.

245. Galston interview.

246. Clinton, *Living History*, 258.

247. Clinton, *It Takes a Village*, 138.

248. Ibid.

249. Clinton, *Living History*, 260.

250. Ibid, 261.

251. Ibid.

252. Ibid, 259.

253. Ibid, 258.

254. Smith, *For Love of Politics*, 189.

255. Troy, *Hillary Rodham Clinton*, 140.

256. Lissa Muscatine, telephone interview with the author, September 8, 2014.

257. Bernstein, *A Woman in Charge*, 420.

258. Remarks by First Lady Hillary Rodham Clinton at the Ciragan Palace, Istanbul, Turkey, March 27, 1996, transcript, http://www.clintonlibrary.gov/assets/storage/Research-Digital-Library/flotus/muscatine-flotus-press/Box-018/2011-0415-S-flotus-statements-and-speeches-6-1-95-4-26-96-binder-ciragan-palace-istanbul-turkey-3-27-1996.pdf.

259. Hillary Rodham Clinton, Address to the Asia Pacific Economic Cooperation Women and the Economy Summit, September 16, 2011, http://video.state.gov/en/video/1183537005001.

260. Hillary Rodham Clinton, Address to the Rajiv Gandhi Foundation, New Delhi, India, March 29, 1995 (Office of the Press Secretary, The White House).

261. Todd S. Purdum, "Hillary Clinton Finding a New Voice," *New York Times*, March 30, 1995.

262. Hillary Rodham Clinton, email message to the author, May 11, 2015.

263. Clinton, *Living History*, 279.

264. Ibid, 280.

265. Ibid, 281.

266. Muscatine interview.

267. Hillary Rodham Clinton, Address to the United Nations Fourth World Conference on Women, September 5, 1995, http://www.un.org/esa/gopher-data/conf/fwcw/conf/gov/950905175653.txt.

268. United Nations, "The Universal Declaration of Human Rights," http://www.un.org/en/documents/udhr.

269. Clinton, *Living History*, 306.

270. Patrick E. Tyler, "Hillary Rodham Clinton, in China, Details Abuse of Women," *New York Times*, September 6, 1995.

271. Jan Piercy, telephone interview with the author, August 12, 2014.

272. Alyse Nelson, telephone interview with the author,

October 2, 2014.

273. Clinton, *Living History*, 341.

274. Ibid, 362.

275. Ibid, 413.

276. Verveer interview.

277. Hillary Rodham Clinton, "Talking It Over," December 13, 2000, http://clinton4.nara.gov/WH/EOP/First_Lady/html/columns/2000/Mon_Dec_18_112032_2000.html.

278. Melanne Verveer, email message to the author, January 28, 2015.

279. "First Lady Hillary Rodham Clinton Speaks at the Democratic National Convention," transcript via PBS News, http://www.pbs.org/newshour/bb/politics-july -dec96-hillary-clinton/.

280. Clinton, *It Takes a Village*, 89.

281. Ibid, 237.

282. Ibid, 92.

283. Ibid, 196.

284. Robert Dole, "Address Accepting the Presidential Nomination at the Republican National Convention in San Diego, August 15, 1996." The American Presidency Project, http://www.presidency.ucsb.edu/ws/ ?pid=25960.

285. Clinton, *Living History*, 369.

286. Lissa Piercy, telephone interview with the author, August 22, 2014.

287. Ibid.

288. Nancy Wanderer, telephone interview with the author,

September 26, 2014.

289. Ibid.

290. Sheehy, *Hillary's Choice*, 39.

291. Hillary Rodham Clinton, *An Invitation to the White House: At Home with History* (New York: Simon & Schuster, 2000), 341.

292. Producer interview with Kenneth Starr, online content from "Clinton," *American Experience*, season 24, episodes 3 and 4, directed by Barak Goodman, aired February 20–21, 2012, http://www.pbs.org/wgbh/americanexperience/features/interview/clinton-starr.

293. Clinton, *Living History*, 245.

294. Ibid, 297.

295. Ibid, 331.

296. William Safire, "Blizzard of Lies," *New York Times*, January 8, 1996, http://www.nytimes.com/1996/01/08/opinion/essay-blizzard-of-lies.html.

297. Clinton, *Living History*, 335.

298. Ibid.

299. Bernstein, *A Woman in Charge*, 484.

300. Susan Schmidt, Peter Baker, and Toni Locy, "Clinton Accused of Urging Aide to Lie," *Washington Post*, January 21, 1998, page A1.

301. Clinton, *Living History*, 441.

302. Ibid, 445.

303. Smith, *For Love of Politics*, 309.

304. Ibid, 300.

305. "A Chronology: Key Moments in the Clinton-Lewinsky

Saga," CNN.com, http://edition.cnn.com/
ALLPOLITICS/1998/resources/lewinsky/timeline.

306. Ann O'Leary, telephone interview with the author, August 1, 2014.

307. Clinton, *Living History*, 466.

308. Ibid.

309. Ibid.

310. Ibid, 469.

311. Ibid, 479.

312. "The Extraordinary Hillary Clinton," *Vogue*, November 6, 2009, http://www.vogue.com/1800443/from-the-archives-the-extraordinary-hillary-clinton.

313. Ibid, 471.

314. Clinton, *It Takes a Village*, 57.

315. Bernstein, *A Woman in Charge*, 25–26. (Italics in the original.)

316. Paul Tillich, *The Shaking of the Foundations* (New York: Charles Scribner's Sons, 1955), "Chapter 19: You Are Accepted," online content prepared by John Bushell, http://www.religion-online.org/showchapter.asp?title=378&C=84.

317. Clinton, *Living History*, 472.

318. Ibid, 489.

319. Ibid, 471.

320. Ibid, 494.

321. Mary Dejevsky, "I Still Love Bill Despite His Weaknesses, Says Hillary Women," *The Independent*, August 2, 1999, http://www.independent.co.uk/news/world/i-still-love-bill

-despite-his-weaknesses-says-hillary-women-1110268.html.

322. Gerth and Van Natta Jr., *Her Way*, 199.

323. Clinton, *Living History*, 502.

324. Ibid, 501.

325. Gerth and Van Natta Jr., *Her Way*, 205.

326. Clinton, *Living History*, 501.

327. Ibid.

328. Gerth and Van Natta Jr., *Her Way*, 207.

329. Ibid, 208.

330. Piercy interview.

331. Kolbert, "The Student."

332. Josh Getlin, "Hillary Rodham Clinton Formally Announces Senate Campaign," *Los Angeles Times*, February 7, 2000.

333. Letter from Amity Weiss to Hillary Rodham Clinton, January 5, 2000.

334. Clinton, *Living History*, 506.

335. Adam Nagourney, "It's Official: First Lady Is Now Candidate Clinton," *New York Times*, February 7, 2000.

336. Frank Buckley and Phil Hirschkorn, "Hillary Rodham Clinton reflects on anniversary of Senate campaign," CNN, July 7, 2000, http://cgi.cnn.com/2000/ALLPOLITICS/stories/07/07/hrc.anniversary.

337. Clinton, *My Life*, 931.

338. Clinton, *Living History*, caption of photograph 75 before page 367.

339. Gerth and Van Natta Jr., *Her Way*, 228.

340. United States Senate References, Featured Books,

"*Citadel* by William S. White," http://www.senate.gov/
reference/reference_item/Citadel.htm.

341. Kolbert, "The Student."

342. O'Leary interview.

343. Ibid.

344. Joshua Green, "Take Two: Hillary's Choice," *The Atlantic*,
November 2006, 4.

345. O'Leary interview.

346. Muscatine interview.

347. Lissa Muscatine, email message to the author, January 27,
2015.

348. Gerth and Van Natta Jr., *Her Way*, 226.

349. Clinton, *Living History*, xiii.

350. Gerth and Van Natta Jr., *Her Way*, 230.

351. Clinton, *Hard Choices*, 172.

352. Ibid.

353. Joshua Green, "Take Two: Hillary's Choice," 5.

354. Clinton, *Hard Choices*, 173.

355. Remarks by President George W. Bush on Iraq,
Cincinnati Museum Center–Cincinnati Union Terminal,
Cincinnati, Ohio, October 7, 2002, http://www2.gwu
.edu/~nsarchiv/NSAEBB/NSAEBB80/new/doc%2012/
President%20Bush%20Outlines%20Iraqi%20Threat
.htm.

356. Senator Hillary Rodham Clinton, "Hillary Clinton Iraq
War Full Speech 10/10/02 Part I," YouTube video, 9:59,
posted by "janetrogers6," October 2, 2007, https://www
.youtube.com/watch?v=4wyCBF5CsCA.

357. Ibid.

358. "Hillary Rodham Clinton Talks Politics and Future,"
     interview with Katie Couric, *Dateline* (NBC), April 16,
     2004, http://www.nbcnews.com/id/4757422/ns/dateline_
     nbc-newsmakers/t/hillary-clinton-talks-politics-future/#
     .VHzMA1fF800.

359. "Hillary: 'I'm In, and I'm In to Win," YouTube video,
     1:50, posted by "PoliticsTV.com," January 20, 2007,
     https://www.youtube.com/watch?v=xvyRN9ka5Fw.

360. Ibid.

361. Amy Chozick and Maggie Haberman, "Hillary Clinton
     to Announce 2016 Run for President on Sunday," *New
     York Times*, April 10, 2015, A10.

362. Gerth and Van Natta Jr., *Her Way*, 304.

363. Ibid, 330.

364. Dan Balz, Anne E. Kornblut, and Shailagh Murry,
     "Obama Wins Iowa's Caucuses," *Washington Post*,
     January 4, 2008, http://www.washingtonpost.com/wp
     -dyn/content/article/2008/01/03/AR2008010304441
     .html?sid=ST2008010400230.

365. Jon Meacham, "Letting Hillary Be Hillary," special issue,
     Newsweek, January 21, 2008, 31.

366. "Clinton's 'Likeable Enough?'" online video clip from
     Meet the Press (NBC), http://www.nbcnews.com/video/
     meet-the-press/44893688#44893688.

367. Jennifer Parker, "Clinton Gets Emotional on Campaign

Trail," ABC News, January 7, 2008, http://abcnews.go
.com/blogs/politics/2008/01/clinton-gets-em.

368. "Hillary Tears Up During Campaign Stop," YouTube
       video, 1:58, posted by "Veracifier," January 7, 2008,
       https://www.youtube.com/watch?v=6qgWH89qWks.

369. Gerth and Van Natta Jr., *Her Way*, 340.

370. Jennifer Parker, "Clinton Wins in N.H.: I 'Found My
       Voice,'" ABC News, January 9, 2008, http://abcnews
       .go.com/Politics/Vote2008/story?id=4103339&page=1.

371. Peter Baker and Anne E. Kornblut, "Even in Victory,
       Clinton Team Is Battling Itself," *Washington Post*, March
       6, 2008, http://www.washingtonpost.com/wp-dyn/
       content/article/2008/03/05/AR2008030503621_4
       .html?sid=ST2008030600084.

372. "On the Record." CBS News. March 25, 2008.

373. Clinton, *Hard Choices*, 1.

374. Parker, "Clinton Gets Emotional on Campaign Trail."

375. Muscatine interview.

376. Alexandra Jaffe, "Hillary Reflects on 2008 Loss: 'I Didn't
       Have a Very Good Strategy,'" The Hill, June 9, 2014,
       https://thehill.com/blogs/ballot-box/presidential-races/
       208760-clinton-reflects-on-2008-loss-i-didnt-have-a
       -very-good.

377. Clinton, *Hard Choices*, 3.

378. "Hillary Clinton Endorses Barack Obama," transcript,
       New York Times, June 7, 2008, http://www.nytimes.com/

2008/06/07/us/politics/07text-clinton.html.

379. Ina Jaffe, "Clinton Exits Race, Vows to Fully Support Obama," NPR News, June 7, 2008, http://www.npr.org/templates/story/story.php?storyId=91282297.

380. Clinton, *Hard Choices*, 8.

381. Patrick Healy, "Clinton Rallies Her Troops to Fight for Obama," *New York Times*, August 27, 2008, http://www.nytimes.com/2008/08/27/us/politics/27dems.html.

382. Hillary Rodham Clinton's Democratic Convention Speech, transcript, *New York Times*, August 26, 2008, http://www.nytimes.com/2008/08/26/us/politics/26text-clinton.html.

383. Clinton, *Hard Choices*, 10.

384. Jan Piercy, August 12, 2014.

385. Clinton, *Hard Choices*, 137.

36. Hillary Clinton, interview with Diane Sawyer, ABC News, June 5, 2014, http://abcnews.go.com/Politics/hillary-clinton-interview-21-revealing-quotes/story?id=24064953.

387. Ibid.

388. Ibid.

389. Jaffe, "Clinton Exits Race, Vows to Fully Support Obama."

390. Clinton, *Hard Choices*, 15.

391. Ibid, 18.

392. Ibid.

393. "Nomination of Hillary R. Clinton to Be Secretary of State, Hearing Before the Committee on Foreign

Relations," January 13, 2009, http://www.gpo.gov/fdsys/
pkg/CHRG-111shrg54615/pdf/CHRG-111shrg54615.pdf.

394. Allen and Parnes, *HRC*, 85.

395. Kim Ghattas, *The Secretary: A Journey with Hillary
Clinton from Beirut to the Heart of American Power* (New
York: Henry Holt and Company, 2013), 12.

396. Clinton, *Hard Choices*, 21.

397. Ibid.

398. Ghattas, *The Secretary*, 21.

399. Hillary Rodham Clinton, book tour speech on publication
of *Hard Choices*, Long Center, Austin, Texas, June 20,
2014.

400. Clinton, *Hard Choices*, 45.

401. Ibid, 43.

402. Clinton, Address to the United Nations Fourth World
Conference on Women.

403. Ghattas, *The Secretary*, 45.

404. Clinton, *Hard Choices*, 82.

405. Hillary Rodham Clinton, email message to the author,
May 11, 2015.

406. Ghattas, *The Secretary*, 49.

407. Ibid, 49.

408. Clinton, *Hard Choices*, 79.

409. Ibid, 41.

410. Ibid, 80.

411. Muscatine email.

412. Allen and Parnes, *HRC*, 141.

413. Ibid, 233.

414. Clinton, *Hard Choices*, 191.

415. Ibid, 193.

416. Ibid, 194.

417. Ibid, 195.

418. Allen and Parnes, *HRC*, 238.

419. Clinton, *Hard Choices*, 197.

420. Text from a postcard from the Clinton Presidential Center.

421. Allen and Parnes, *HRC*, 326.

422. Clinton, *Hard Choices*, 86.

423. Muscatine interview.

424. Steven Lee Myers, "Emails Expand on Mosaic of Secretary Clinton's Days," *New York Times*, August 1, 2015.

425. "On-the-Record Briefing by Secretary of State Hillary Rodham Clinton," Embassy of the United States: Seoul, Korea, February 19, 2009, http://seoul.usembassy.gov/ p_sec_022009c.html.

426. Ghattas, *The Secretary*, 115.

427. Allen and Parnes, *HRC*, 135.

428. Clinton, *Hard Choices*, 529.

429. Clinton, *Hard Choices*, 378

430. Ibid, 392.

431. Allen and Parnes, *HRC*, 301.

432. Hillary Rodham Clinton, interview with Christiane Amanpour, CNN, June 17, 2014.

433. Allen and Parnes, *HRC*, 367.

434. Ibid, 362.

435. Ibid, *HRC*, 339.

436. Ibid, 367.

437. Allen and Parnes, *HRC*, 374.

438. Ibid, 365.

439. Hillary Rodham Clinton, interview with Christiane Amanpour, CNN, June 17, 2014.

440. "U.S. Government Action Plan on Children in Adversity: A Framework for International Assistance, 2012–2017," http://www.childreninadversity.gov/about/how/action-plan.

441. Anastasia Ordonez, "White House Word Gap Event to Share Research & Best Practices with Aim to Close Word Gap," http://thenextgeneration.org/blog/post/white-house-word-gap-event-to-share-research-best-practicies-with-aim-to-cl.

442. Hillary Rodham Clinton, "Hillary Rodham Clinton: Job One for America: Putting Young People to Work," *Denver Post*, Guest Commentary, June 24, 2014, http://www.denverpost.com/opinion/ci_26025717/job-one-america-putting-young-people-work.

443. Karen Tumulty, "Hillary Rodham Clinton Announces 'No Ceilings' Initiative to Empower Women," She the People, *Washington Post*, November 1, 2013, http://www.washingtonpost.com/blogs/she-the-people/wp/2013/11/01/hillary-clinton-announces-no-ceilings-initiative-to-empower-women.

444. Geetika Rudra via *Good Morning America*, "Clintons Tweet Out Baby Pictures," September 27, 2014, http://abcnews.go.com/US/hillary-clinton-moon-grandmother/

story?id=25806524.

445. Hillary Rodham Clinton, email message to the author, May 11, 2015.

446. Ibid.

447. "Gains and Gaps: No Ceilings Data Visualization," YouTube video, 2:12, posted by "Bill, Hillary & Chelsea Clinton Foundation," September 24, 2014, https://www.youtube.com/watch?v=ebG_k9XoshI.

448. Clinton Foundation, "Inspiring Girls to Empower Others," October 11, 2014, https://www.clintonfoundation.org/blog/2014/10/11/inspiring-girls-empower-others.

449. Raymond Hernandez, "Hillary Clinton Takes the Stage, and the Speculation Heats Up," *New York Times*, June 13, 2013, http://www.nytimes.com/2013/06/14/us/politics/hillary-clinton-steps-onto-a-stage-again.html.

450. Hillary Rodham Clinton, interview with Christiane Amanpour, CNN, June 17, 2014.

451. Liz Kreutz via *Good Morning America*, "Hillary Rodham Clinton Defends High-Dollar Speaking Fees," June 9, 2014, http://abcnews.go.com/Politics/hillary-clinton-defends-high-dollar-speaking-fees/story?id=24052962.

452. Hillary Rodham Clinton, email message to the author, May 11, 2015.

453. Ibid.

454. Hillary Rodham Clinton, interview with Christiane Amanpour, CNN, June 17, 2014.

455. Hillary Clinton, "A New Chapter," Huff Post Politics, April 11, 2015, http://www.huffingtonpost.com/hillary-

clinton/hard-choices-epilogue_b_7037880.html.
456. "Getting Started," video, 1:35, posted April 12, 2015, https://www.hillaryclinton.com.
457. Clinton, *Living History*, 41.

BIBLIOGRAPHY

Sources of information about a woman who has largely lived her life in public for the past forty years are almost endless. The following abbreviated list comprises the major works to which I referred while researching and writing this book. Additional sources can be found in the notes.

Allen, Jonathan, and Amie Parnes. *HRC: State Secrets and the Rebirth of Hillary Clinton*. New York: Crown Publishing Group, 2014.

Bernstein, Carl. *A Woman in Charge: The Life of Hillary Rodham Clinton*. New York: Vintage Books, 2008.

Clinton, Hillary Rodham. *Hard Choices*. New York: Simon & Schuster, 2014.

———. *An Invitation to the White House: At Home with History*. New York: Simon & Schuster, 2000.

———. *It Takes a Village: And Other Lessons Children Teach Us*. New York: Simon & Schuster, 1996.

———. *Living History*. New York: Simon & Schuster, 2003.

Gerth, Jeff, and Don Van Natta Jr. *Her Way: The Hopes and Ambitions of Hillary Rodham Clinton*. New York: Little, Brown and Company, 2007.

Ghattas, Kim. *The Secretary: A Journey with Hillary Clinton from Beirut to the Heart of American Power*. New York: Henry Holt and Company, 2013.

Horn, Miriam. *Rebels in White Gloves: Coming of Age with Hillary's Class—Wellesley '69*. New York: Crown Publishing Group, 1999.

Radcliffe, Donnie. *Hillary Rodham Clinton: The Evolution of a First Lady*. New York: Grand Central Publishing, 1999.

Smith, Sally Bedell. *For Love of Politics: Inside the Clinton White House*. New York: Random House, 2008.

INDEX